Getting Through the

DARK DAYS *of* CAREGIVING

SECOND EDITION

CAROL NOREN PATTERSON

Getting Through the Dark Days of Caregiving, Second Edition

This book is written to provide information and motivation to readers. Its purpose is not to render any type of psychological, legal, or professional advice of any kind. The content is the sole opinion and expression of the author, and not necessarily that of the publisher.

Copyright © 2021 by Carol Noren Patterson.

All rights reserved. No part of this book may be reproduced, transmitted, or distributed in any form by any means, including, but not limited to, recording, photocopying, or taking screenshots of parts of the book, without prior written permission from the author or the publisher. Brief quotations for noncommercial purposes, such as book reviews, permitted by Fair Use of the U.S. Copyright Law, are allowed without written permissions, as long as such quotations do not cause damage to the book's commercial value. For permissions, write to the publisher, whose address is stated below.

Printed in the United States of America.

ISBN   978-1-953150-78-3   (Paperback)
ISBN   978-1-953150-79-0   (Digital)

Lettra Press books may be ordered through booksellers or by contacting:

Lettra Press LLC
30 N Gould St. Suite 4753
Sheridan, WY 82801
1 307-200-3414 | info@lettrapress.com
www.lettrapress.com

*In memory of 101-year-old
Virginia Uptrain who passed away
during the 2020 pandemic
when I could not go visit her*

TABLE OF CONTENTS

Acknowledgements vii

Introduction ix

Chapter 1 Alzheimer's And Dementia 1

Chapter 2 Changing Roles 11

Chapter 3 Biggest Issue I Faced 22

Chapter 4 Problem Behaviors Of Dementia Patients 40

Chapter 5 Caregiving Stress 56

Chapter 6 Loving The Care Receiver 75

Chapter 7 What Others Can Do 89

Chapter 8 Activities for Care Receivers 99

Chapter 9 Dying Realities 106

Chapter 10 Grief 122

Epilogue 141

Books Cited and Consulted 155

Further Resources 161

"Carol writes from the trenches. If you are in the battle with Alzheimer's, you will identify with her. I know, I have been there. If you are not in the battle but anticipating it, walking with her will help you prepare. You will find hope as Carol points you to the only source of hope on this journey--Jesus Christ and the grace that flows from him."

Dr. Howard Eryich
Former Pastor of Counseling Ministries
Briarwood Presbyterian Church
Birmingham, Alabama

"The one word that sums up Carol's book on care giving for Alzheimer's and other forms of dementia is "practical." Whether citing research on dementia care giving or citing the experience of others in dementia care giving or relating her own story, the emphasis is on practicality. She seeks to answer the questions, what actually works in dementia care? What can I do to help my loved one enjoy the safest, most meaningful life possible? And how can I take care of myself and get through today? Sometimes practical help is inspiration and encouragement from music or poetry or the Bible. And that is included too. Anyone looking for practical, useful information on dementia care will find Carol's writing helpful."

Rev. Carl Malm
Center for Loss, Grief and Change
An Interfaith Ministry of the Huntsville Association for Pastoral Care

ACKNOWLEDGEMENTS

Chris Wilcox is a professional counselor with the Alzheimer's Association, and has led me through the process of dealing with the hurts and joys of caregiving; he helped me decide between Hospice and a nursing home for my late husband Herb Johnson. Stefanie Thompson Wardlow was my Florida Alzheimer's Association Support Group facilitator who gave me much insight and support. Biblical counselor Dr. Howard Eyrich has offered invaluable help along the way. He and his wife were also caregivers for his father who had Alzheimer's. Dr. Eyrich, your belief that I could take on this writing challenge has inspired me. Grief counselor Rev. Carl Maim helped me process grief as I wrote the tenth chapter.

The late Kenneth Sexton was a natural caregiver who had stayed in a nursing home for two years with dementia patients; he volunteered for my husband Herb and came to church with us. Kenny even traveled with us. Day in and day out he saw my best and my worst and advised me. Numerous friends and family members partnered with me in prayer and received my text messages requesting prayer. Sally and her husband Jake (who has Alzheimer's—not their real names) did many things with Herb and me. Sally and I are in regular contact now as she struggles with Jake.

Thanks to Georgene Girouard, and Gay Finkelman who early on offered valuable editing suggestions and encouragement. I could not have managed the stress of being a caregiver, subsequent widowhood while writing this

Acknowledgements

book, without my having friends sitting by my computer figuratively, if not physically. Karl and Carol Freels, you came along at the right time during my widowhood to encourage my completion and added invaluable insight by suggesting and attending meetings at the library; later the Freels confirmed that this project should be a book, not a dissertation, and prayed with me about a book. Thanks to Delena Loughmiller who kept me going towards the completing of this project. Thanks to the colloquium of pastors and professionals who helped me brainstorm what the church can do. Special thanks to Huntsville Health and Rehabilitation Center where, for the almost three weeks I, as a patient, lived among dementia patients.

Thanks to Dr. Kenneth G. Talbot for my introduction to biblical counseling in Lakeland, Florida with the Whitefield Seminary course work begun in the fall of 2006 and completed in the spring of 2013, during my caregiving for my late husband. Thanks for allowing me to teach the class "Counseling Children", and for suggesting the topic for this project, at first a dissertation idea, and now a book. Thanks for advising me all along as my pastor with half of my fourteen-year marriage devoted to caregiving. Thanks for the dissertation suggestion that has also become a book in its second edition and for the honorary doctorate awarded in 2021 in time for this second edition.

Above all, my LORD Jesus Christ, whom I long to see. There will be no more tears in heaven. We will dance there.

INTRODUCTION

This book is autobiographical, practical and theological. It covers strategies to help Christian counselors, pastors and caregivers, and friends to minister to the needs of care receivers. Behaviors of dementia care receivers are detailed, as are strategies for caregiver stress and facing the mourning that follows the death. Chapters one, three and four are for dementia and Alzheimer's caregivers. The other seven chapters are for all caregivers including dementia caregivers.

One's life journey is one surprise after another—losses of various sorts and degrees. Marriage hands each spouse many joys and surprises of all sorts. In addition, marriage in the senior years can be a test of commitment as each spouse faces difficulties and health issues in the journey of aging. Some of those surprises may include the demands and care of aging parents, or for some, such as myself, the care of a spouse. Dementia and Alzheimer's are certainly one of the issues with numerous challenges. I have been blogging about my Herb Johnson's mixed dementia, Vascular Dementia (Vascular Cognitive Impairment) and Alzheimer's, writing up interviews and Alzheimer's research at Plant City Lady and Friends blog since December of 2008. I wrestled with all sorts of issues in my new role as a caregiver for my late husband. I have read widely about dementia, but have realized there are issues that demand a Christian perspective and hence this book.

Certainly we want a cure for Alzheimer's, yet a definite cure may not be on the horizon; should a cure be discovered, there will still be care receivers who have contracted dementia

Introduction

to be dealt with. In the meantime, I am writing for clergy and laypeople, caregivers and their counselors, widows and widowers left alone when the disease takes their spouse, family members who grieve for the years lost and final death of their family member, deacons, parish nurses, Stephen's Ministers and wonderful friends and neighbors who attend the last days of the care receiver's life. Care receivers haven't chosen their disease and its most common form of Alzheimer's disease. However, our loved ones deserve the best care for God's glory.

> *For God is not unjust to forget your work and labor*
> *of love which you have shown toward His name,*
> *in that you have ministered to the saints.*
> **Hebrews 6:10**

CHAPTER 1

ALZHEIMER'S AND DEMENTIA

Summer 2018 I walked to the checkout at a supermarket and looked at the magazines. This one caught my eye: **The Essential Guide to Caregiving.** *Ten years ago I could have used this magazine when my husband was first diagnosed with dementia,* I reflected as I checked out my groceries. My husband Herb Johnson died June 23, 2014 and this book is what I would now tell others—spouses, adult children of dementia patients, and all who care.

A New Kind of Death

In 1967, S. I. McMillen's book, *None of These Diseases,* was first published. McMillen looked at what the Bible had to say about health and diseases. Dementia and Alzheimer's were not even mentioned in his book. He mentioned smoking as a cause of heart disease and cancer.[1] Dr. McMillen noted these statistics on causes of death of men who regularly smoked[2]:

---

[1] Excerpt from p.85 of None of These Diseases by S. I. McMillen, copyright © 1963, used by permission of Revell, a division of Baker Publishing Group.

[2] Ibid., p. 31.

- Coronary Artery Disease—52%
- Lung Cancer—13.5 %
- Other Cancer—13.5 %
- Other Heart and Circulation—5.8 %
- Pulmonary—5.6 %p
- Cerebral Vascular—4.8 %
- Gastric and Duodenal Ulcers 2.8 %
- Cirrhosis of Liver—1.5 %
- All Other—4 %

That was some fifty years ago. *The Better Homes and Gardens Family Medical Guide* a few years later does not have a definition for Alzheimer's Disease, but does define dementia vaguely as "metal deterioration, usually implying serious impairment of intellect, irrationality, confusion, stupor, 'insane' behavior," and goes on to say it "may result from poisons, physical changes in the brain, toxins produced by disease, or psychoses of which the basic cause is unknown."[3] In 1997 author Roy Porter notes that Alzheimer's is one of the conditions that has grown rapidly in wealthier nations.[4]

So now we have caregiver magazines in the supermarket checkout stands that used to feature Psychology Today. We have fewer smokers, but we have new statistics with how people die. There is less death from AIDS. There is less cancer and heart disease, and more Alzheimer's and dementia as the population ages. U. S. News reports that 5.1 million Americans now are affected by Alzheimer's.[5] That same article goes on to report:

---

[3] Cooley, Donald G., editor, *Family Medical Guide*, (NY: Better Homes and Gardens Books, Penguin, 1973), pp. 920-921.

[4] Porter, Roy, *The Greatest Benefit to Mankind: A Medical History of Humanity* (NY: W. W. Norton & Co, 1997) p. 29.

[5] Costa, Samantham, "Fear and Hope: Life After Alzheimer's Diagnosis", *U.S.News*, 1/20/16, http://health.usnews.com/health-news/health-wellness/articles/2016-01-20/fear-and-hope-life-after-an-alzheimers-diagnosis.

The disease often labeled as an "old" person's disease affects approximately 5.1 million Americans over 65, and roughly 200,000 people under 65 have the early-onset type of Alzheimer's disease. One in 9 people older than 65 has Alzheimer's disease. The number of Americans 65 and up with the disease and other dementias is expected to increase 40 percent to 7.1 million by 2025, according to the Alzheimer's Association's 2015 Alzheimer's Disease Facts and Figures Report.

For one state:

> Experts say that as Florida's population continues to age such specialized facilities will be even more in demand. The Alzheimer's Association predicts that 720,000 Floridians will be diagnosed with the disease by 2025, a 44-percent increase over 2015 estimates.[6]

Alzheimer's and dementia need a definite diagnosis from a neurologist or from a geriatric psychiatrist. A medical doctor can and often does confirm dementia with an oral test; however, it's common knowledge that many seniors want to keep their doctors from discovering their dementia. The patient can be depressed and misdiagnosed with Alzheimer's. Rosalynn Carter writes:[7]

> Depression among the elderly is often misdiagnosed. In some cases, the confusion and memory loss associated with it can be mistaken for Alzheimer's disease or "senility." If depression

---

[6] Inman, Jessica, "Memory care communities respond to increase in Alzheimer's", 1/21/16, http://www.orlandosentinel.com/health/os-memory-care- communities--20151231-story.html.

[7] Carter. Rosalynn, with Susan L. Golant, *Helping Someone With Mental Illness: A Compassionate Guide for Family, Friends, and Caregivers* (NY: Random House, 1998), pp. 64-65.

Chapter 1

> is truly the cause of these symptoms, it can be reversed with proper treatment. Alzheimer's, the slow deterioration of brain function eventually leading to death, will not improve with therapy, but treatment can enhance an Alzheimer's sufferer's quality of life and coping skills.

Mrs. Carter's book deals with helping family and friends with mental illness, but the realm of caregiving for dementia sufferers has unique features and challenges. Unlike mental illness, a cure for most dementias has not been discovered except for a few conditions such as Vitamin B12 deficiency.[8] Again a proper diagnosis is needed.

Terms

Alzheimer's is the most common form of dementia. Dementia has been described as the umbrella term.

> Dementia is an umbrella term, a general term covering many different diagnoses. In fact, there are over 75 types of dementia. The term dementia refers to a group of symptoms that affects functioning in everyday life. Symptoms can include memory loss, impaired judgment, difficulties with language and attention, and personality changes.[9]

The estimate is that 60 % of dementia is Alzheimer's[10].

---

[8] Help Guide. Org., "What's Causing Your Memory Loss?" n.d. http://www.helpguide.org/Harvard/what's-causing-your-memory-loss.htm#reversible9
[9] Heltemes, Monica, "What is Dementia? Is it the Same as Alzheimer's" 6/24/14, http//:www.mind-start.com/difference between Alzheimer's-and-dementia.html?
[10] Ibid.

The **caregiver** is the one who takes care of the **care receiver**. Often the care receiver is the loved one (spouse, parent, sibling or even church friend). That caregiver becomes the world for the person with the disease; he or she explains what is happening because life makes less sense to the dementia sufferer.

The **church** includes the pastors, counselors, deacons, Stephens Ministers[11], parish nurses and regular church members—the body of Christ. Luke 14:37 says individuals and their families may want to bear their own cross, but at some point, the disease will probably involve outside help. Stronger believers are called upon to "bear with the failings and the frailties and the tender scruples of the weak and to help carry the doubts and qualms of others" according to Romans.[12] The apostle Paul told the Galatians simply that they were to bear one another's burdens.[13] At times this will mean a simple chore of daily living that others can help with, but at other times it will mean putting up with the distasteful behaviors that come along with dementia.

The church comes along side to support the caregiver and the care receiver, and this effort will be enormously costly emotionally, physically, financially and spiritually. We can only look to our LORD Jesus Christ who is seated on the right hand of the Father to intercede for us in this trial of watching and helping others who are going through this disease, a result of the fall of man.[14] We can walk away from caregiving, or we can become a caregiver. Caregiving for my late husband Herb changed me.

General Observations on Caregiving

The challenge of caregiving is daunting. Caregiver groups with the Alzheimer's Association or within the church can help the caregiver identify and apply these observations.

---

[11] See resources.
[12] Romans 15:1 Amplified
[13] Galatians 6:2
[14] Genesis 3

Chapter 1

1. Communication skills need to change. Noted Christian author and counselor H. Norm Wright is often quoted as saying: "It's been suggested that successful communication consists of 7 percent content, 38 percent tone of voice, and 55 percent nonverbal communication. We're usually aware of the content of what we're saying, but not nearly as aware of our tone of voice."[15] This implies:

2. Do not argue. Sometimes you have to agree and then change the subject.

3. At times you have to take the blame because no amount of explaining will work.

4. The calendar is a great tool because what you say needs also to be put in writing on a clipboard or on a wipe-off board. Establish this procedure early in the disease when your loved one can be trained to use a white board or calendar.

5. You cannot seem bossy, even though you realize you must be in charge.

When I moved to Huntsville, Alabama after Herb died, I met an almost 100-year-old Virginia who had lost her sight, but she was as sharp as a tack and remarkably interesting to talk with; she became my prayer warrior and she added "confidant". I would say, I want to be just like you when I am your age! We had both buried two husbands. I would say to my dog Ziggy, do you want to go visit Miss Virginia and he would get all excited and we would go see her. I would lift him up on her bed and he would lick her!

Offer the illusion of control. Nobody likes to feel as though the decision maker is ordering them around all of the time—and

---

[15] H. Norm Wright, https://www.goodreads.com/author/quotes/27559.H Norman Wright

this applies especially to people with dementia. If caregivers communicate in a way that makes loved ones feel they no longer can make their own decisions, anger follows. The reality of dementia is that, as reasoning and judgment diminish, caregivers must take more control and make hard decisions. However, it's possible to communicate with loved ones in ways that give them a semblance of control.

All these adjusted ways of communicating mean that the caregiver often does not feel at home in the situation. The adjustments are tremendous. The apple cart is upset. But for the husband with dementia, for example, his apple cart is also upset and he needs his wife to make sense of the world for him. He still has personality, likes, dislikes and unique motivations. He is still there. He lives in the moment, not appreciating much of recent days and not looking forward to tomorrow. Many of the couple's family and acquaintances have little idea how impaired he is, as he seems fairly normal to them.

When bouts of stress, frustration and depression take a toll on the health of a caregiver, the friends, church and family can play an increased supportive role.

1. It is important to get a Living Will and a Durable Power of Attorney and to decide who will become the health surrogate. If you wait too long, becoming a Legal Guardian is enormously complicated and expensive.

2. Becoming an Alzheimer caregiver is the most difficult job one can have, with anticipatory complicated grief, feelings of guilt and premature unavoidable detachment from the loved one. Caregivers are encouraged to take breaks for their own mental health. Peter Rabins writes:

   > Caregivers should try to recognize and accept the fact that feelings of love for a relative may be tempered with anger, anxiety, frustration, or embarrassment. These reactions are perfectly

natural and should not be a source of guilt. Caregivers should consider joining a caregiver support group and should try to schedule regular respites. It's important to ask for help, set realistic goals, and consider professional counseling if necessary. Exercise is important for mental and physical health.[16]

Thibault and Morgan write that there is medical and legal help, but not the emotional and spiritual support needed.[17]

3. Research is ongoing and a research study may help. Nutrition does have an important impact.

4. Roles switch.

Roles are distinct from responsibilities, which are the jobs people do. Roles refer to positions that someone assumes within the family, be it as parent, spouse, homemaker, decision-maker or advice-giver. Roles are established over many years, making them a little more difficult to transfer from a loved one to you. . . .Children often hesitate to decide personal matters for a parent, for example, moving from a private home to assisted-living quarters . . . These changes require emotional adjustments. As awkward and uncomfortable as you may feel, you must come to terms with the fact that people with dementia, even at an early stage of the disease, will need someone to step in and help them with certain tasks and with certain

---

[16] Rabins, Peter V., *The Johns Hopkins White Papers: Memory 2010* Baltimore, MD: Johns Hopkins Medicine, 2010), pp. 58-59.

[17] Thibault, Jane Marie and Richard L. Morgan, *No Act of Love Is Ever Wasted: The Spirituality of Caring for Persons with Dementia* (Nashville, TN: Upper Room Books, 2009), p. 19, used by permission.

decisions. Even if your loved one seems resentful or angry with your help, you're responding to the demands that the disease has placed on both of you.[18]

Some families are in what has been called "the sandwich generation" where they are caring for young and old.[19]

5. Financial Expense. Medicine such as Namenda and Exelon is enormously expensive. Hospice is available for the presumed last six months of care upon the doctor's orders.

6. The person with dementia doesn't need to know the diagnosis or may not remember it. They need reassurance. Be there for them. Do not deceive them, but it is not necessary to tell them all that the disease involves.

7. Not everyone will understand the situation, but even from a distance they can help. The Mayo Clinic suggests: Even if you live far away, your support can be critical to a primary caregiver's ability to function and cope. Stay in frequent contact by telephone or e-mail. Send cards and letters of support. Try to visit and offer some respite, if that would be helpful. Ask the caregiver to inform you of situations where he or she could use assistance. Perhaps the most important way you can support the caregiver is to avoid passing judgment on his or her decisions. Listen closely and ask questions about the situation, but don't assume you know everything that's happening. Your emotional support and encouragement are integral.[20]

---

[18] Petersen, Ronald, Medical Editor in Chief, (*Mayo Clinic Guide to Alzheimer's Disease* (Rochester, MN: Mayo Foundation for Medical Education and Research, 2006), p. 231.

[19] Lamm, Benjamin, "The Sandwich Generation", n. d. http://blog.caregiverpartnership.com/2015/04/the-sandwich-generation.html

[20] Petersen, op. cit., p. 234.

Chapter 1

The challenge is huge, but the church can help members in the congregation bear the burdens of dementia and caregiving. We can love one another this way. More strategies follow and suggestions for how pastors and counselors can help practically. Above all remember to pray for one another.

CHAPTER 2
CHANGING ROLES

Dementia becomes a family and a church family problem. Some pastors are not equipped to handle these issues because they did not receive that training in seminary. Roles are reversed within the family and the church family calling for much wisdom.

Honoring Parents With Dementia

Taking care of a parent with Alzheimer's can be a huge challenge.[21] What becomes evident is that the adult child has to step in to care for an ailing parent. With mobile populations this is not always possible and often nursing homes are a necessity.

Rev. Greg Asimakoupoulos had a mother with dementia, and he penned this poem.

When the Parent Becomes the Child

When I was but a boy of three,
my mother took good care of me.
She cooked my food and washed my clothes

---

[21] Marley, Marie, "When the Tables Are Turned and You Become the Dementia Parent," 7/7/14, http://www.alzheimersreadingroom.com/2014/07/when- tables-are-turned-and-you-become.html, used by permission.

Chapter 2

> and dressed me for the day.
> She helped me tie my laces tight
> and tucked me in my bed at night.
> She put my needs ahead of hers
> and never once complained.
> When I fell down or lost my way,
> my mom was never far away.
> She recognized my helpless state
> and made me feel secure.
> But now my mom's "the child" in need
> who struggles daily to succeed
> at little tasks that tax a mind
> that frequently forgets.
> She needs my help to get around
> or look for things until they're found.
> And when her eyes betray her fear,
> I hold her trembling hand.
> At times her needs can drain me dry,
> but when I start complaining why?
> I think back to my childhood
> and how she cared for me.[22]

No small task it is to switch roles.

In the Old Testament, Noah became drunk and his sons respectfully handled the situation reported to them by Ham: *But Shem and Japheth took a garment, laid it on both of their shoulders, And went backward and covered the nakedness of their father. Their faces were turned away, and they did not see their father's nakedness.*[23]

When a disease such as dementia strikes, the children will indeed need to step in and solve problems. The parents are not

---

[22] Asimakoupoulus, Greg, http://plantcityladyandfriends.blogspot.com/2012/07/ when-parent-becomes-child.html, poem used by permission.

[23] Genesis 9:23

their former selves, but their dignity needs to be maintained—as Ham maintained Noah's dignity.

Certainly the family dynamics change. It is best to keep the lines of communication open, but also to expect that some adult children will not be able to handle their parent's disease; perhaps they do not live near the parent. Perhaps they have enough to handle with their own lives. The responsible sibling may resent that he/she is carrying more than the "fair share" of the load. However, there should not be resentment or guilt placed on any one.

The Alzheimer's Reading Room blog offers these valuable suggestions from the Mayo Clinic:

> Share Responsibility: Families who do function well often split the caregiving duties among the various family members to avoid placing all the responsibility on the primary caregiver. For example one person may do the actual caregiving while others assume tasks such as handling the finances or helping out by doing errands or chores.
>
> Meet Regularly. Meet Face to Face Regularly: It's important for family members to meet and discuss the situation on a regular basis. (When one or more family members lives out of town, you may try using Skype.) It can also be helpful if the primary caregiver makes detailed lists of the patient's dementia symptoms. These lists should be updated frequently and shared with everyone on a regular basis in order to educate the others about the loved one's condition.
>
> Ask Someone to Mediate, if Necessary: Both Larkin and the Mayo Clinic recommend engaging the services of a mediator when all else fails. It can be helpful to involve a neutral third party.

You can find qualified mediators on the website of the Academy of Professional Family Mediators. You can also talk to trained personnel at the Alzheimer's Association (24/7) at 1-800-272-3900.

Be Honest and Don't Criticize: As is the case when dealing with any type of conflict, all family members should be honest about their feelings and try to avoid criticizing the others.

Consider Counseling: The Mayo Clinic advises that if the conflict is serious enough try joining a support group or even getting family counseling. It can be helpful to share your difficulties with others in the same situation or, again, engaging the services of a neutral third party.[24]

There are many challenges when the adult children do not live near the parent, but with established modes of communication for input from others this can be managed. Should the distant relative be judgmental, it might be necessary to cut off communication for the time being. Few people can understand the shoes in which the primary caregiver walks. The caregiving role also can become a blessing in the end especially if shared and appreciated by the family and others in the church.

---

[24] Mare Marley,"What to Do When Alzheimer's Threatens to Tear Your Family Apart", *The Alzheimer's Reading Room*, n. d. http://www.alzheimersre adingroom.com/ 2014/06/ Alzheimers-dementia-Family- Conf lict.html?utm source= feedburner&utm medium=feed&utm campaign=Feed%3A+ TheAlzheimers ReadingRoom+%28Alzheimer%27s+Reading+ Room%29, used by permission.

Wife Under Husband's Authority

In biblical terms, the husband is to be the head of his wife as Christ is to be the head of His church.[25] His headship is a given in the marriage and a delight to the wife. Proverbs says that the husband trusts his wife and that she *does him good all the days of her life*.[26] For Christians who follow Scripture both the wife with a husband who has dementia or the husband with a wife who has dementia have undoubtedly vowed to love *in sickness and in health until death us do part*.

What about the marriage where the husband has been the head of the home and where he now lacks judgment and may not even recognize or trust his wife as the disease progresses. Dr. Jay Adams, who regularly has answers to these and other biblical or nouthetic counseling questions referred to his colleague Dr. Howard Eyrich. Eyrich suggested that there are in fact biblical examples of female leadership that depart from the biblical norm. [27]

- Book of Judges when women take up leadership.
- Nabal's wife when her husband makes foolish decisions (his name means fool) and her action is rewarded.
- Also, when Lyddia was converted, it appears that she took up leadership for the initial start up of the church.

In other words, the norm is not absolute. Adjustments can be made when contingencies require it.[28] Dr. Eyrich explained that just as male headship is the norm, one can look at authority as a "continuum." The wife shifts to coming more under the direct authority (shepherding) of elders who in turn give the caregiver much more latitude in execution with their oversight.

---

[25] Ephesians 5:21 ff; Colossians 3:18, 19; 1 Peter 3:1ff and Titus 2:3-5
[26] Proverbs 31:11-12
[27] Interview of Howard Eyrich, email, recorded in Whitefield Seminary paper, 8/29/2010, used by permission.
[28] Ibid.

Chapter 2

Examples of the need for the wife to take over include finances and safety. A husband can begin to spend money that doesn't fit into the budget. A husband may want to drive beyond his own safety and the safety of others. He may begin to hallucinate and the wife may need to remove his prized gun collection from the home.

Spousal Caregiving

When the husband is caring for his wife, and really any spousal caregiving will be a challenge.

I gave up full-time teaching, which meant financial strain. My husband controlled the TV programs. I do not know what to watch now that I am no longer a caregiver watching TV with my late husband— not that TV matters. But in so many ways I was blessed having my church family and interaction with Sally and her husband.

One journalist, Barry Peterson, decided when his wife no longer remember him, that it was permissible for him to have another partner. As a Christian I totally disagreed and posted a review.[29]

> In reading Jan's Story I discovered it is really BARRY'S STORY of how he copes with his wife Jan's Early Onset Alzheimer's. Jan becomes angry, confused and has friends who aren't there. She hardly recognizes Barry at the end of the story while Barry becomes lonely and overburdened with her care.
>
> What did I as a caregiver learn from this caregiver/correspondent? Barry chronicles the stages of

---

[29] Carol Noren Johnson, "Jan's Story by Journalist Barry Petersen," 7/1/2011, http:// plantcityladyandfriends.blogspot.com/2011/07/jans-story-by-journalist-barry- petersen.html

Alzheimer's as Jan goes through them. He writes to family and friends in the summer of 2007:

"I am taken aback at how fast Jan's short term memory seemed to evaporate . . . it robs us of sharing daily experiences, and robs her of savoring the good things that are a part of all of our daily lives . . . I am losing more than a friend . . . also slipping away is the one person who was my confidante, with whom I could and did share everything. I feel like I'm trapped in a movie, watching it unfold and already know the ending . . . but with no way to rewind back to the good parts."

So much is familiar in Jan and Barry's story--having to order for my husband in restaurants, his misplacing things, his compensating for memory loss, sundowner's problems. Barry talked about Jan's coping experiences--ANGER, PRETENDING, SILENCE. But my husband hasn't deteriorated as much as Jan has by the end of the book.

While I respect Mr. Petersen and his riveting journey as a caregiver, his values do not represent my Christian values. I did not see Mr. Petersen looking to the Lord for strength and guidance in his caregiver's story. He brings a third party (not the Lord), a new woman into the story for his loneliness. Barry seemed to find people to support his new woman while his wife is in assisted living. Even Jan's mother suggested Barry needed a side romance!

I am a caregiver who takes a different path. I have a different view of fidelity and an awesome God

> who is with me in this journey. Life doesn't owe me a husband. I married for the first time when I was 40 and when that husband died I was a widow for eight years. I love being married to my husband and we have so much joy in our marriage. Life doesn't guarantee a husband not get Alzheimer's. But I do have this chance to be faithful to my husband and be the best wife I can be while the Lord takes me through this.

Dementia is no excuse for the caregiver to commit adultery, even if he or she is not even recognized by the spouse. You are in your marriage for better and for worse, in sickness and in health.

Friedman's Triangle

How can counselors work with families of dementia sufferers? Edwin Friedman has written a most helpful book, *Generation to Generation*.[30]

He developed **the responsibility triangle**.

> The problem is that we cannot make another family member responsible by trying to make him or her responsible. The very act of trying to make others responsible preempts their own responsibility. This is equally true whether the issue is study habits, drinking, or failure to come to church There is, however, a way to be our brother's keeper, to manifest responsibility for a fellow human being without getting stuck in a triangle between that person and his or her failure to be responsible. It is called "challenge," but it requires one to non-anxiously tolerate pain, and sometimes even to

---

[30] Friedman, Edwin H. *Generation to Generation: Family Process in Church and Synagogue,* (NY: The Guilford Press, 2011).

stimulate pain, thus forcing the other to increase his or her threshold.[31]

He lists five concepts in his "Family Systems Theory". The **first** concept is to identify **who** has the problem in the family/congregation; that person is part of a system what responds to the problem. With dementia patients, it is often others that can be dealt with, not the patient himself or herself. Friedman writes:

> A major consequence of this distinction is that family therapy should not be confused with what has been traditionally understood as "family counseling." In the later, family members are seen in order to help them cope with a problem in another family member. But that only reinforces the labeling process. Family therapy, instead of simply trying to calm the family, tends to treat crisis as an opportunity for bringing change to the entire emotional system, with the result that everyone, and not just the *identified patient*, personally benefits and grows.[32]

Solutions can be found within this family system.

The **second concept** is "homeostasis" or balance. The family or congregation wants things to remain as they always have been. However, the disease of dementia will not change. Friedman goes on to point out that the emotional system of the church or synagogue has almost the same intensity and does certainly influence one another.

"Differentiation of self" is the **third** concept. Changes in one member can help the whole system and bring new homeostasis. It is the caregiver for the patient that needs coaching and support to bring out family strengths. This person is the adult child or the

---

[31] Ibid., p. 49
[32] Ibid., p. 23.

spouse most usually, although close friends or extended family members can step into the role.

The **fourth** concept is extended families, which often present problems in blended families—who will be in charge.

The **final** concept is the emotional triangle. Friedman explains:

> The basic law of emotional triangles is that when any two parts of a system become uncomfortable with one another, they will "triangle in" or focus upon a third person, or issue, as a way of stabilizing their own relationship with one another. A person may be said to be "triangle" if he or she gets caught in the middle as the focus of such an unresolved issue.[33]

The key for the counselor is to maintain a well-defined relationship with both parties. The minister, counselor, doctor or policeman can tell a patient that it is time to give up driving much more effectively than can the caregiver. That authority is not part of the triangle of the relationship. Thus it is the loving action to bring in a party that can help without emotion.

To explain family systems theory related to dementia, Friedman offers this helpful example. Mrs. O'Connor is a church member who has come to her minister for help with her mother who is in the throws of memory problems and cannot be trusted to live alone. Rather than the triangle of the pastor being caught in the middle of the mother and Mrs. Connor, he helps Mrs. Connor set boundaries *one marked by the ability to say a very determined "no" but with a smile that also said "I love you."* [34] There will be those situations where the caregiver needs to be proactive such as noted in a blog post when I prevented my husband from

---

[33] Friedman, op. cit., pp. 35-36.
[34] Ibid., p. 156.

driving off.[35] The pastors and counselors can be those catalysts for change without getting caught in the middle.

Godly Counsel

Caregivers and church leaders with caregiver ministries for their deacons need to find their own solutions with God's help and he has promised to guide. Remember:

a. Ask God for wisdom (James 1:5).
b. *God has not given us a spirit of fear, but of a sound mind* (2 Timothy 1:7). Ask for a sound mind when dealing with your AD loved one.
c. Realize that *all things work together for good* according to Romans 8:28. This life is not all and we do not need the Hollywood ending to the story. We will grow in grace as we accept the role of caregiver.
d. The caregivers need to control their anger. Do not return *anger for anger, an eye for an eye.*[36]
e. Realize that others do not walk in the caregiver's shoes and need to be forgiven as Christ has forgiven us when others misspeak or do not understand.

We are called to bear our own burdens, but when the burden is great as with dementia caregiving, we need to bear one another's burdens and not grow weary.[37] Skillfully the pastor or counselor becomes the one to help the caregiver effectively solve problems. More on how the church can help with bearing burdens of caregivers in chapter seven.

---

[35] Carol Noren Johnson, "Saga Twenty-Five", 5/31/2012, http://plantcityladyandfriends.blogspot.com/2012/05/saga-twenty-five.html
[36] Proverbs 14:29
[37] Galatians 6:2; 2 Thessalonians 3:13

CHAPTER 3
BIGGEST ISSUE I FACED

Every patient and caregiver has different concerns. While stopping my husband's driving concerned me quite a bit (people could die or he could wander), his guns were my biggest concern. With hallucinations he could use them! What if he killed someone with a gun?

My late husband Herb always wanted to know what's "on tap" for the day.

"I have an errand this morning and maybe we can go to Shoot Straight later," I say. *I have been putting off going to the shooting range at least four months, and am hoping someone else will go with him—three men that like my husband and know he has stage one Alzheimer's. What is it with men and guns!*

I ask my husband if he would like to come on that errand with me. I have to bring a document to a part-time employer in Lakeland. He says yes and suggests we take our dog.

Taking Ziggy involves putting him in a harness, extra small, and putting the seat belt through his harness in the center back seat. Ever since our accident when my small Saturn was totaled and our lives were spared due to our seat belts, we decided that Ziggy would be in a doggy seat belt arrangement in the middle of the back seat. While I am in the car and while we are driving, Ziggy does stay put and safe.

I put my purse, a notebook, my iPod for music through the car speaker and a book in the front seat. Hubby may have one thing on his mind (driving), but I always have to read a book or an article while he drives. Conversation is not always productive with hubby as he proudly concentrates with his excellent driving skills and my directions for getting us someplace. The three of us back out of the garage in our gas-guzzler.

He starts out driving. "I always think of Jake," he says. Our friend Jake did not pass the Alzheimer's driving test, but hubby did last fall. "I will study the book before my next exam," hubby says. That exam will be in maybe two months. We head south on Highway 39 and notice a sign says we cannot take the Sam Allen/Park Road route to Lakeland.

Well into our half-hour errand, I say that I have forgotten the document. I had been reading my book.

"Lady, you take the cake and I'm the one with the . . . what is it?" "Short-term memory," I say.

We need gas and on the way back home I help him with directions to get around the block to the gas station. I jump out to pay and pump and he rolls down the electric windows. Putting the card in at the pump can be confusing for him and he tells me I might as well pump today too. Ziggy sees me at the pump and stays put in his seat belt.

Nearby a car radio is loud. "I want to shoot that guy," hubby says. Guns and Alzheimer's patients. Thoughts race through my mind. Alzheimer patients (more disabled than my husband at this stage) are known to shoot someone they no longer recognize. Their anger comes from missing neurons in the hippocampus part of the brain. Realizing this a year ago our pastor took the weapons to sell—all but the 45 gun, hubby's prized gun. But the guns weren't sold and people saw that my husband was actually doing quite well. The guns waltzed back into the home with pastor's instructions to get locks for them or to lock them up. We had a carpenter install a lock on the guest bedroom for this purpose. The 45 had been missing for several weeks, and since I had been busy teaching a counseling class, I hadn't taken time to look for it. One day we even opened the popup camper to

Chapter 3

look for it. I knew it wasn't in there, but hubby was determined it could be.

Then came that Saturday when we argue about the 45. He wants to go out and buy another 45 and I didn't agree. I want to find the missing one that I was sure I had stashed away. He tells me I am an obstinate and rebellious woman. We yell at each other, not something I can ever remember doing before. "Hang in there with me until Monday," I request. "On Monday I will look for your 45 and if we can't find it we will go out and buy another one." Monday came and I am depressed all day as I tear the house apart. I recall his accusation—"obstinate and rebellious" woman. I cannot find the missing gun.

Monday night we go out and trade one of his guns in for a new 45. They gave us $175 for a Ruger pistol and we buy a $589 SPG 45. I feel the peace return to my marriage. We spent money we really should not have spent. I watch my husband fill out the forms and the clerk check his concealed weapon permit. They take time to do a background check of some sort which cost us $5. He passes. There is room on the credit card for the purchase. No one checks to see if my husband has Alzheimer's— he just appears slow filling out forms. That next day when I was looking in a bin in the guest bedroom, I find the missing 45 that I had hidden in the locked up-room. Now we have two of these darn guns!

Going back home to get the document I had forgotten, hubby asked, "Where do I get off [I-4] now?

"Highway 39," I tell him since he remembers that Park Road is closed. *Mmm, I think. His memory is good here.*

Approaching the house he quips, "I will give you one more chance and if you don't get that document, you are going to have to walk home!" I laugh. Love his humor. He adds as we drive up to the house, "Ziggy, what are we going to do with mama's memory?"

I go in the front door from our circular driveway. Escape artist that he is, Ziggy is out of his extra small harness. *Both my hubby and my dog think they have to be ready to rescue me—hubby by going with me on errands and often driving and Ziggy by following me when he can. Ziggy must think he can crash through the car window to rescue me if needed.*

After all three of us are back in our seat belts and I have the document, we pull out of the circular driveway and hubby says, "We need to do something about. . ."

"The weeds." I finish his sentence. He doesn't mind if I finish his sentences these days.

"It's gonna take both of us," he says and I agree. I had neglected the yard this summer while I taught that graduate class. He had barely kept up with mowing the yard.

I put my "Oldies" playlist from my iPod on in the car. We hear again "Side by Side", our song. *Oh we ain't got a barrel of money/ Maybe we're ragged and funny/ But we' ll travel along, Singing our song/ Side by Side/ Don't know what's coming tomorrow. . . .*

Park Avenue is blocked and we approach I-4 from the north. There are signs all around.

"Which one?" he wants to know. "Take the Orlando on-ramp."

Hubby enjoys the beat of the oldies music. I remind him to get off at the Memorial exit.

"Stay on Memorial for a long time and then turn at Wabash. You know, by that gas station where the guy played loud music."

"Don't give me a lot of useless information," he snaps. I keep forgetting that he can only handle one direction at a time.

We get to the destination and I go inside a two-story building with my document. Hubby and Ziggy remain in the air-conditioned car with motor running on our gas guzzler. Inside I deliver my document and chat with employees about the Power Point and song I will put together for a going-away party.

When I return from the building, Ziggy is out of his extra small harness and I fasten him again. It is noon and I ask Hubby if he would like Wendy's for lunch. He says yes and with a long line of cars I am dispersed to go inside and buy our lunch. I get him chicken nuggets, French fries and a small frosty—he always trusts me to order these days. Really a choice on a menu

Chapter 3

is difficult for him as with other Alzheimer's loved ones. It's always, "You know what I like."

Back in the car, with Ziggy harnessed and belted up again, we head home. As we approach Plant City, I say "Don't get off this turn. Take the next one." It was two ideas, but he seemed grateful for the directions.

The rest of the day I love being home and tying up loose ends. It is so restful. No pressure. Soon I will substitute teach many days to pay for things like guns, reducing credit cards and save for the future when I can't work and need to be a full-time caregiver. Hubby does his usual watching old movies on cable TV or on his DVD player in the family room.

About nine o'clock he comes to the den and says, "You'll love going to the shooting range with me. We will both have 45 guns to use." I fume inside!

I rise at 5 AM before the alarm clock and go to the den to read my daily Scripture. I write e-mails to ladies I have never met, but these dear ladies regularly write on my blog and we pray for each other. Today will be the day when hubby goes to the shooting range. Just before the alarm goes off at 6:15 I go back to our bedroom where hubby is talking to dog Ziggy. I need to leave by 8 AM to substitute teach 24 minutes away in a school I rarely sub at—English and Reading, my certifications.

I remind my husband that Wayne is picking him up to go to the Shoot Straight after lunch. We start to get his bag ready for shooting with his original 45. I give hubby a check and mark on the check's memo hubby's yearly membership to Shoot Straight. The new 45 is put away and I hope to sell it, but this is not his idea. One by one I bring boxes of ammo to him so he can look for 45 bullets. He has A LOT of ammo. What was he ever thinking? Then I return each box of ammo to the locked bedroom where his other weapons are kept. His stuff is confusing to him and he swears.

I find two sets of earmuffs from when we went to the Shoot Straight together before the Alzheimer's--one for Wayne and one for Herb. *I do not want to have anything to do with shooting any more.* He asks again who Wayne is.

"Your ex brother-in-law." "When is he coming?" "After lunch—one PM."

"Will you pick me up to go to the shooting range?" "No! I will meet you there."

"How will I get there?"

"It's on the clipboard." That clipboard originally was his idea and on days I am gone I have a detailed schedule printed on it. Yesterday when I was gone he did not check things off on it; however he managed breakfast and lunch—but no morning pills.

I take my shower, I start to dry my hair and put makeup on. I bring hubby his pills and breakfast to his spot in the family room where he watches TV or DVDs. The coffee table has his DVDs, some videocassettes, his clipboard with schedule, and Kleenex. Under the table is a small wastebasket. If my husband doesn't have his pills with his breakfast, he vomits into this wastebasket when he swallows the pills later. I always wish he would eat breakfast and have his pills before I leave home. HAVE PILLS WITH FOOD, is on that clipboard. Also on the clipboard are two questions he has to ask me: *Did Carol take her pills? Did Carol feed Ziggy?* He asks and I say thanks and he checks these off. Actually I put my pills in a small container to swallow as I drive to school.

I start loading the car—iPod for podcasts I listen to in the car, cell phone to call hubby when I get to school and when I am free to call, my pink bag that contains puzzles for students, a book for me to read if I get a chance and my umbrella. And the pills and the thin bagel with salmon cream cheese.

On the trip I eat my bagel and swallow my pills—*certainly don't want to take my pills in the classroom. The students may think I am on something! They will soon think I am crazy enough if I do one of my raps for them.*

One by one the curlers come out and I fling them in the back seat. I have to stop for school buses, but enjoy the ride through strawberry fields in various stages of preparation for next winter's crop. I notice one country home with two stories

Chapter 3

and two-story porches on three sides. *Why is that interesting house painted orange?* I wonder.

Nearing school I call my husband to tell him I have arrived at the destination. In the classroom I have forgotten to turn off my cell phone and I get a call from hubby in the classroom.

"Where are you? When will you be home?"

"I am teaching in class now, Sweetheart. I will see you at the range. Check the clipboard," I say.

I have to hang up. He understands.

"Bye," he says.

I do call at lunch when I can talk. I remind him that Wayne will be coming and to have his lunch.

The students took a writing pretest. One student asked, "Does this test count for a grade?" *Everything counts in life*, I think. *The clipboard counts. Will that clipboard continue to work? When will I need to stay home full-time and stop substitute teaching?*

After school I check for messages on my cell. Hubby had gone to Wayne's house. I drive there happy that he had an outing with a guy. When I arrive at Wayne's home, I found out that my husband had bought a $300 one-year membership at the shooting range for both of us—not just for himself! He also wants to buy lasers for both of our 45 guns! We go to dinner at Sweet Tomatoes with Wayne.

When we arrive home, I ask my husband, "Did you have a good day with Wayne?"

"What did we do?" he asks.

Another day is the tenth anniversary of what has become known as "9-11" when the New York World Trade Towers came down and other events happened in the United States. My husband watches this on the news Sunday morning and tells me he wants me to drive to church because he is sad. Usually he drives on Sundays.

The next day my husband asks: "What's on tap for today?"

"You are mowing the front yard this morning and I am tying up loose ends. This afternoon we go to our couples support group at the Alzheimer's Association in Eloise." Today there is no printed schedule on the clipboard because I am with hubby all day.

"So what are you going to be doing all day?"

"I am going to be with you all day."

"So what am I worried about?" *My husband is very dependent on me.*

He is exhausted and hot after mowing the front yard. I remind him we need to leave for Eloise at 2 pm.

"I'm not going," he says.

"I told you this morning that we had this date. I cancelled myself from substitute teaching because of this support group." He decides to take a shower and will go if I drive. We are going with our friends Sally and Jake to a special Alzheimer's support group for couples. We somehow get there on time. Mary Jo, a Memory Care Specialist, is our substitute facilitator today. She says she has never had a group where there are both caregiver and their Alzheimer's loved one. One Alzheimer's patient has an art activity while his 81-year-old caregiver wife is in the group along with Paula, Evelyn and Chet. We all have our turns talking. Caregiver Chet reminds the group that 60 % of caregivers die before their loved one. Chet's wife says she guesses her daughter would take care of her if Chet were to die. With characteristic humor my husband says to me that he would kill me if I die first!

I tell Mary Jo this support group experience has helped us as a couple talk about this Alzheimer's journey we are on. Then I bring up my topic.

"Honey, do you remember the day we argued about buying a gun?"

"No," he says.

Mary Jo says that you never ask someone with dementia if they *remember* something. She has other good reminders:

- *Keep to a schedule. You will be glad later.*
- *Keep your loved one safe.*
- To Joann and the husbands: *You won't know if you have poor judgment.*

Chapter 3

- To my husband: *There will come a day when Carol will need to lock up your guns—when you are hallucinating.*

Chet chimes in about not taking those guns away yet. I think to myself: *I have been obsessing about my husband's guns. The LORD will have to protect us.*

Mary Jo sums up the session emphasizing that the Alzheimer's patient

1. Is in denial.
2. Lacks good judgment.
3. Can't be reasoned with.

After the support group Sally, Jake, Herb and I go to dinner at Olive Garden in Winter Haven and I discover that I don't have my wallet and no driver's license. My husband therefore drives the four of us home. *I will miss his careful driving if he does not pass the Alzheimer's driving test.*

Another day he asks: "What's on tap for today?"

"I have my writing class, Jake is coming over about 1:30 and Sally and I will be at our monthly Alzheimer's Association support group this afternoon. Tonight the four of us will go to dinner. There are leftovers from Olive Garden in the refrigerator for you to warm up."

I should be on time for my Life Writing class at 10 am. The address number is 6150 and I head for Lakeland Hills Boulevard. No 6150 and I check again. *OK it is 6170 Lakeland Highland Boulevard.* I head south and try to leave a message for the facilitator on her cell phone. Leaving a message doesn't seem to work.

When I arrive at the destination at the opposite end of town, there is no meeting. So I check my bag where I had actually printed out the e-mail—1919 Lakeland Hills Boulevard. I turn and head back to where I was. I am late and no one is calling my cell phone. I reflect that I am so discombobulated. This must be what my husband feels about much of his dementia now—**discombobulating fear**. I am the fifth person to arrive there and they are glad to see me.

After class, the multitasker that I am, I go to the Lakeland Post Office to mail two packages. On the way back to Plant City, I check in with hubby: "Did you have lunch?"

"It's in the microwave."

"OK, Sweetheart, please have lunch before Jake comes." At the support session I turn in funds for the local Alzheimer's Walk. We talk about Marjorie whose husband has just died at home. She has had Hospice at the house to help her. Shirley talks about her stage three husband who is now in an assisted living facility. Shirley's husband wants to come home and calls her often. Jack tells of his wife who is miserable now in her assisted living place; she left their home about two weeks ago and he will be moving out because his wife's daughter is in charge of the finances now and she will sell the home. The facilitator reminds Jack and Shirley not to visit their spouse at a predictable time to check on how good the care is. After two productive hours Sally and I leave the monthly support group. I turn my cell phone back on and get a call from hubby. "Where have you been? Jake and I are starving!"

"Sally and I are driving home now."

When I arrive home I discover the secret of the hungry husbands— lunches are still in the microwave. We four leave for Grandpa Johnson's Restaurant on Alexander in Plant City. I drive so Jake doesn't complain about Sally's driving. At the restaurant Sally and I both order for our husbands. Thank you, LORD, for this couple relationship where we bear each other's burdens.

I had been substitute teaching and reading a book called, *The Excellent Wife*. I saw a billboard in Lakeland that said the gun show was the 16th and the 17th. Convicted that hubby wants in his heart to go to one and buy a laser attachment for his 45, I bring up the gun show. I look it up on the Internet. Those dates were for last year. This year's Lakeland Gun show is November 5 and 6 and those lasers are cheaper at the gun show. I suggest we go there in November to get one for his Christmas gift. He likes

Chapter 3

that. No longer is he obsessing about guns. I do remind him that Mary Jo said there may come a day when I have to lock this up, especially if he is hallucinating. He says he will know before I do when that day is. *Yet Mary Jo reminded us all that an Alzheimer's patient doesn't have good judgment.*

I made myself unavailable to substitute teach so we could go to Sally and Jake's church for their monthly senior's event. Everybody brought a bag lunch and a collectable hobby to share. Sally was in charge and so she had me perform some of my raps for the group. Sally shared her antique trays, Jake—his birdhouses, hubby his toy horse collection. I shared four items from my ruby red glass collection.

Usually pills and breakfast will happen after I leave the house, when hubby gets his false teeth in. He needs to eat something when he takes those pills and three days last week he ate breakfast, but no pills while I had to leave to substitute teach. Saturday when I was off to teach a first-time driver's class, I had a plan for those pills. Put them on the plate with his breakfast, because putting the pillbox by his breakfast doesn't cut it. Great solution.

Alzheimer's patients need socialization and hubby loves to get out. Wednesday night we went to Toastmasters, the club that I helped form at a church in Lakeland. I tend to talk too much there—go over my time limit, but when my husband is called on for "Table Topics" at Toastmasters his verbal skills are excellent—often humorous and to the point with this extemporaneous exercise.

But are his verbal skills really excellent? I love his prayers, but I realize that he now uses limited vocabulary and concepts when he prays at night. He thanks God for the "good" day and goes on about the "good" day, without specifics of what happened, for maybe four or five sentences.

He can ask me questions successfully (many times it is the same question up to six times), but he cannot respond to my queries. For example, I spilled milk on the dining room carpet and wanted him to bring me towels quickly.

"What kind?" he wants to know. "Paper towels?"

"No. Hurry and get towels out of the basket on the pink trunk in our bedroom." That was too much information for him. I ended up getting the towels and as it was Sunday morning and we had to leave for church, I wouldn't be able to clean that carpet.

What about his reading skills? He doesn't always like to read the daily clipboard schedule I make for him. He has another pad that he writes on to supplement that daily schedule. He will then cross off the item after it has happened. He reads the bulletin and hymns in church, but doesn't read so much during the week. There came a time when my blogging friend Dolores's husband stopped reading—something her husband dearly loved to do. Hubby loves to watch videos and so far that is what he does while I am off supplementing our income.

Social Sunday Night. We get home from church activities about 4:30 and get ready for guests to come at 7 pm for another pool night at our home. Three gentlemen and Sally and Jake's delightful ten year old granddaughter play pool while we three wives play Mexican Dominos. The granddaughter starts enjoying our dog Ziggy, who also liked the attention. My husband and Jake sit in the family room to watch TV while Bob goes to the den ready to keep score. Now hubby doesn't realize as a host he needs to be playing pool. I remind him and like Archie Bunker in the old TV comedy, hubby shushes me up. About five minutes later the two Alzheimer's husbands join Bob in the den where the granddaughter has fun playing with three old men.

"Sally," I quip as we ladies play our domino game, "do you realize your granddaughter is learning to enjoy playing pool with men?"

It is so great that our two husbands are taking turns playing with two others who keep track of the game. Good week, but verbal skills are declining I realize.

I can substitute every day and then work on Saturday. Not good for hubby. I decided to make myself unavailable to substitute at least once a week and let the LORD take care of us financially and me spiritually. I will have more time to be **WITH**

Chapter 3

my husband, so important. We book going to the shooting range. At dinner at TGIF we discuss this outing. "I forget what you shoot with," my husband says. *He does not remember he wanted me shooting with the extra 45. Maybe I can sell it.*

"We will figure it out," I assure him. "Do you still want that laser attachment for your birthday?"

"That's a good idea he says." The gun show is in November and his birthday is in December. My husband wants very little--no clothes, maybe DVDs. I tell him I want a Kindle or a Nook for Christmas. He says that I should work it out in the budget. Hubby mostly wants to be **WITH** me.

October 2011 "Shoot Straight" Shooting Range. My husband doesn't even ask what is "on tap" for the day. He has remembered. He has patiently waited for me to go to the range with him. This is the day. *Mary Jo, he is not hallucinating yet.* He calls me into the bedroom. *He has remembered we have two 45 guns because he gets both out.*

"Tell me at the shooting range how to use them," I say. "See if you can get the lawns mowed before we go." I thank the LORD for giving me the grace to go on this date with hubby. Never thought I would. I kept fighting guns because they are dangerous for later stage Alzheimer's patients.

A promise is a promise. Ziggy gets a treat when he goes to the bathroom outside. I take him outside, but he stays on the deck. We come back in and he expects a treat.

"No treat, Ziggy. You didn't pee outside," Herb says training Ziggy. Am I training the Alzheimer's husband? Or is he training me? Today he will train me to use that extra 45 that I had wanted to sell.

Hubby starts watching "Walk the Line," one of his favorite movies. No teeth in for breakfast and pills and no plans to mow the lawn. Lyrics Johnny Cash sings in this DVD: *My momma told me, sonny, don't ever play with guns.* I go on with household tasks. Love having the day off. I worked six days last week to supplement income and I am still suffering a cold and a rotator cuff injury. When the movie is done hubby has decided we will go out. It is 11:30 and he takes a shower, shaves and puts his teeth in.

Hubby drives to Cracker Barrel Restaurant with my direction. I order water and he orders unsweetened ice tea. We often amuse ourselves in a restaurant by blowing the paper off the straw. I am not successfully with my try at blowing off the straw cover, but my husband says "zee master" about his blowing skills and sure enough successfully blows his straw cover at me. We order the $5.99 lunch special for Tuesday.

"Did I put sweetener in my tea?" he asks.

"No, there would be paper from the sweetener on the table if you did," I remind him.

"Do we have guns in the car?"

"Yes, you put them there."

He goes to the restroom, and I wonder if he can find his way back to the table. He does this time. We enjoy our meatloaf and side dishes. At least five times he asks where we are going next.

"To Shoot Straight."

I direct him how to get to Shoot Straight. We have a $300 yearly membership there—hubby's dream for our dates for the next year. I have been there before—before the Alzheimer's and he was thrilled I would go there with him. We were also there to buy the 45 gun to replace the one he thought he had lost. When we get to the desk, the Shoot Straight employee says, "How nice, father and daughter shooting together!" I don't think hubby heard that, or he didn't react to what was said. I gulped!

We put our earmuffs on and go into the target area. Hubby forgot to bring his target paper and so I go out to buy some large ones. We begin shooting—each with our own 45 guns now.

Suddenly my husband leaves and goes out to watch me through the windows. Standing and lifting the gun was too hard for him he says. He comes back and we pack up, sweeping the bullet casings and depositing them in the bucket that Shoot Straight provides for this purpose.

Chapter 3

Now $800 has been spent. If he had asked me several months ago, we would not have pursued this hobby. Defeat? No! Victory. The Lord is training me.

We have answered the training question. I train the dog and the Lord trains me through my hubby. You can't argue with an Alzheimer's patient, we are told. It wouldn't have been so easy if I had not been reading Martha Peace's *The Excellent Wife*. Because of Martha and with the Lord's help, I will not be bitter. I will be kind, tenderhearted and forgiving. We leave Shoot Straight without a nagging wife saying "I told you so!"

"Where next?" he asks.

"Office Depot. You want me to drive now?"

"Yes—you drive." He loves to be with me. After Office Depot we go to Barnes and Noble to check out the Nook. There hubby sits and eats in the coffee shop and I have the leisure of discussing the pros and cons of Kindle and Nook. I ask my husband if we can get an early Christmas gift for me—a Nook. He says *yes*. I get the $89 one, the first model that has come down in price. If I had been stewing, I bet the Nook would not have happened. I ask if he still wants the laser for his gun, and he says *no*!

It is after five PM and we start home. Sally calls on my cell phone. She has had a rough day and wants to have dinner with us. I remember after our car accident calling her about the rough day we had and we four also went out to eat. Thank God for this friendship! We meet at Old Time Pizza. Enjoyable.

"Why didn't you invite me to the shooting range?" Jake asks. Sally diverts the question. With Jake's depression she had put his weapons away—given them to their son, I believe. She whispers to me about her worry of Jake's taking his life when he is down. Another Alzheimer's facilitator has told me privately that I should disable my husband's 45. When we get home hubby puts his 45 away in the bedroom. He will only use it in a home invasion he now says. It is loaded. He shows me where he will keep it. He knows about our talk on the subject of hallucinations. I now have all ammo and the other guns locked up in the guest bedroom. I will lock that one gun up when needed. Lord help me. Thank you, Lord that hubby has stopped obsessing about guns now. Hubby again puts "Walk the Line" on to watch for the second time.

He says that "Walk the Line" and "Fireproof" are his favorite movies. We just saw "Courageous" on Sunday and I bet when it comes out he will like it as well. Movies need easy plots for my husband, and he will see them multiple times now.

The next day my husband has thought about Shoot Straight. "I think I am allergic to something in the room where we shoot. Maybe we can go to an outdoor range." I tell him I am not sure how this would work into our budget.

Eventually I was able to sell all of the guns and the ammo except one forty-five, which he kept loaded by the side of the bed.

One night he called to me and said that the gun was under a pillow in the bedroom.

"Well then," I pronounced, "I am NOT going to sleep in our bedroom!"

Ten minutes later he said that it was back in the drawer by the bed. I returned to the bedroom knowing that this weapon would have to leave the house. I sold it to a friend and put Scripture in the drawer that said the LORD would be our protector. He never questioned about that missing 45 and could recall that he no longer possessed weapons.

Three years later, my husband is in another stage of Alzheimer's and it would be in less than year that he would die from the disease. He no longer is driving and hallucinates about evil people.

"I have to buy a gun," he says. He obsesses about the need for a gun to protect us. We go into a Walgreens and I see a police officer; without my husband knowing it, I ask that police officer to please have a talk with my husband because he has dementia and is insisting on buying a gun for protection. A few minutes later I hear the policeman skillfully talk with my husband. Somehow the obsession with guns stopped.

My life changed and I had to discreetly enlist the help of other authorities that the husband may still respect—the doctor, a police officer, a pastor. The wife will have to ask herself if what she now does is biblical and she needs to guard against any idols of her heart in taking over these responsibilities.

Eve was made to be Adam's helpmeet or helpmate. Jay E. Adams defines a helpmate as "a helper who is appropriate for him."[38] She needs to do what is best in the situation, receive counsel from others and pray that her struggles will be a witness to others of Christ's faithfulness. The wife is living out her vows *in sickness and in health, for better for worse, until death us do part.* Because dementia provides enormous challenges for a marriage, solutions need to be evaluated. Jay Adams writes:

> *The solution must be biblical, exegetically based—*
>
> Using Scriptures that rightly apply to the problem, And are carefully understood in terms of their purpose.
>
> *Its outworking must be feasible.*
>
> The suggested implementation must grow out of Scriptural principles.
>
> It must also be consistent with Scripture at all points. *If followed God's way there will be blessing regardless of consequences.*
>
> Obedience does not always lead to pleasant outcomes. But God will bless the outcome in some way.
>
> *And, most important is the honor of God in it all.*

---

[38] Adams, Jay E, *Marriage, Divorce and Remarriage* (Ann Arbor, MN: Cushing-Malloy, Inc., 1980), p. 16, used by permission.

This must be the foremost desire in solving the problem. Determine how to please God by the solution.[39]

Hence it must be noted that the God who has promised to guide us into all wisdom will, as He has in the past, guide in these situations. Mrs. Eyrich brings up the point of common sense. Dr. Eyrich comments:

> I see people become almost paranoid about being sure they are being "spiritual." As my wife often says, "Use common sense." She will then lament, "But common sense is too often in short supply." The reason it is in short supply is because people don't imbibe Scripture sufficiently.[40]

How can the wife be the helpmate to her husband, whom she married, *for richer or poorer, for better or worse, in sickness and health, to death do us part?* The wife will have to become submissive to Him whose providence is superior to all human situations. It is God who will get the glory in this situation as in all situations.

---

[39] Adams, Jay, "Problems/Solutions" 6/3/2010, www.nouthetic.org/blog, used by permission.
[40] Interview of Howard Eyrich, op. cit.

CHAPTER 4

PROBLEM BEHAVIORS OF DEMENTIA PATIENTS

At some point the Alzheimer's patients will most likely display anger, rage, malicious behavior, suspicion, hallucinations, violence, the blaming others and swearing. They have lost their filter because plaques and tangles are taking over their hippocampus in their brain. Because of short-term memory loss, they will ask the same questions over and over or tell the same stories over and over. Their behavior is embarrassing, but excusable. The caregiver perhaps can run interference and explain this behavior to others.

Anger and Aggression

Scripture warns us about anger. We are told in Ephesians to not let anger control us, to *not let the sun go down on your wrath, nor give place to the devil, but be kind and forgiving.*[41] Colossians also spells it out: *You yourselves are to put off all these: anger, wrath, malice, blasphemy, filthy language out of your mouth.*[42] In Proverbs we read: *"He who is slow to wrath has great understanding. But he who is impulsive exalts folly."*[43] Yes, there is righteous anger

---

[41] Ephesians 4:26, 27, 31, 32
[42] Colossians 3:8
[43] Proverbs 14:29

and of course, divine anger, but most often we humans deal in sinful anger. Caregivers dare not get angry in return. Putting on patience is part of our growth. But how can we deal with the anger of someone with a disease? It will be next to impossible to train them.

Two standard books about Alzheimer's do not do justice to the biblical word "anger". *The 36-Hour Day* writes about agitation, irritability, overreacting, and catastrophic reactions. It does make this point, however:

> Anger or violent behavior is usually a catastrophic reaction and should be handled as you would any other catastrophic reaction. . . . Try not to interpret anger in the same way as you would if it came from a well person. [44]

Mayo Clinic Guide to Alzheimer's Disease makes these definitions:

> Agitation involves urgent vocal or motor actions that are disruptive and can be unsafe. Signs of agitation include shouting, complaining, cursing, fidgeting and pacing. Anger is a strong emotional response that often shows itself in a desire to fight back at the cause of displeasure. Becoming irritable is a somewhat milder response.[45]

When the loved one has been diagnosed with Alzheimer's, the whole range of irritability to violence needs to be addressed. Often the term "challenging behavior" is used. For the caregiver, anger is a moral condition that needs confession and repentance,

---

[44] Mace, Nancy L. and Peter V. Rabins, (*The 36-Hour Day*, 4th Edition, Baltimore, MD: The John Hopkins University Press, 2006) p. 153, used by permission.

[45] Petersen, Ronald, Ed., op. cit., p. 282.

Chapter 4

but for the patient anger is a whole different matter--it is part of the disease.

Caregivers and family members have a difficult challenge when faced with these behaviors. Patients with Alzheimer's disease are most often not able to comprehend spiritual counsel concerning their anger and why their anger is upsetting to others. Frequently they cannot remember their anger. Are they morally responsible for their anger? Maybe not. This anger happens because their ability to control behavior gradually fades—they are missing their filter. Take away a privilege or a right to which they feel entitled and they get angry. We have to find out what it is that may be causing their reaction. Their reality is different and they react often to how they are treated. We are the ones that have to deal with their behavior and we need wisdom for the task. The Alzheimer's Association suggests the following:

1. Identify and examine the behavior.

   - What was the behavior? Was it harmful to the individual or others?
   - What happened just before the behavior occurred? Did something trigger it?
   - What happened immediately after the behavior occurred? How did you react?
   - Consult a physician to identify any causes related to medications or illness.

2. Explore potential solutions.

   - What are the needs of the person with dementia? Are they being met?
   - Can adapting the surrounding comfort the person?
   - How can you change your reaction or your approach to the behavior? Are you responding in a calm and supportive way?

3. Try different responses.

- Did your new response help?
- Do you need to explore other potential causes and solutions? If so, what can you do differently?[46]

Pray about what to do with the options at hand. Remember James 1:5 which says, *If any of you lacks wisdom, let him ask of God, who gives to all liberally and without reproach, and it will be given to him.*

It is then left to the caregiver to manage their family member's anger and wrath—behavior usually not seen by people outside the caregiver and family circle. Bob DeMarco of the Alzheimer's Reading Room describes how his mother would be difficult with him, but not with others.[47] The strategy he used was to have his sister call his mother and then his mother would change her mood. Outsiders who don't live day-to-day with the dementia sufferer misunderstand the disease and how anger may play out in the home. Out in public these sufferers are often very polite and charming and do not show challenging behavior. They are on their best behavior.

The home caregivers have to manage anger of the patient, in addition to managing their own stress level for their twenty-four hour seven- day unpaid job. This becomes the time when honoring parents and marriage vows are severely tested. There is no excuse acceptable such as "they are not the person I knew". Caregivers and family are responsible **to** the loved one, but not responsible **for** him.

One day I drove Herb and Jake to our home. Get two gentlemen with Alzheimer's together and there might at long last be an argument after three years of knowing each other. It

---

[46] "Behaviors: How to respond when dementia causes unpredictable behaviors", (Alzheimer's Association, 2010), used by permission.

[47] DeMarco, Bob, https://www.alzheimersreadingroom.com/2015/11/alzheimers- dementia-patients-can-deceive-others.html, 3/22/18, used by permission.

Chapter 4

was bound to happen. Both men are capable of asking the same question over and over again and Sally and I just act like it was the first time it was asked. That day Sally was going to pick up Jake at our home. Later. Jake wanted to know when his wife was coming and kept repeatedly asking every minute or so.

My husband gets mad: *Stop your* [expletive deleted] *asking the same question over and over.*

Jake replies: *Stop you swearing or I will beat you up and never step inside your house again!* He is livid at his buddy of three years.

When we got to our home, Jake goes out to the front yard. I also go out there to see that in his anger at my husband he didn't walk away and wander. I take the hose and started watering the plants. Soon Sally comes to get her angry husband.

Both husbands forget about the incident the next day. Patients do not hold grudges—they can't remember. Alzheimer's and other dementias are not funny, but you just have to laugh sometimes.

Sundowner's Syndrome

Late afternoon and early evening (between 3 pm and 8 pm according to *Learning to Speak Alzheimer's*[48]) the loved one may get especially irritated and act out. This is called Sundowner's Syndrome.[49] This syndrome is not universal for all care receivers, but can be during the early hours as well. Research is being developed to learn more about it.

We do know that early in the disease anger and strange behavior do not happen early in the evening, although in later AD stages they can. Behaviors attributed to sundowners include paranoia, pacing, fear, depression, stubbornness, restlessness,

---

[48] Coste, Joanne Koenig, Learning *to Speak Alzheimer's* (Houghton Mifflin Co, NY: 2003), p. 63, used by permission.

[49] Sundowner Facts.com: A Resource for Sundown Syndrome, n. d. http:// sundownerfacts.com/sundowners-syndrome

rocking, violence, wandering and crying.[50] The patient's sense of day and night disappears. They are also afraid of water also.[51] The strategy for dealing with sundowning is to have a calm pace and provide light in the environment. When I learned about sundowning, I had ceiling lights installed in our family room where Herb spent most of his time. The evening news and violent shows might not be appropriate for the patient because of the content of the news.

Why Does This Problem Behavior Happen?

We can somewhat answer the "why" of anger for the patients. Many other diseases of aging do not include anger. First and foremost, the anger is not always something the patient can control. The hippocampus, which controls social behavior, is losing neurons. Reasoning will not help. That part of the brain is ill. Most often the diseased loved one is not capable of applying Scripture.

One study suggests the dementia loved ones have muted emotions, or flat emotions, which should not be interpreted as depression.[52] We need to do whatever it takes to make them feel emotionally secure so they don't become angry. The loved one misses their driving privileges, for example, and they can obsess about the unfairness of their not being able to drive. Instead, the caregiver needs strategies to deal with the anger of their loved one since the individual cannot control emotions.

We do not expect a mentally or emotionally handicapped person to have the same accountability as someone who does not have a handicap. We can't expect the dementia patient to

---

[50] Sollitto, Mario, "Understanding and Minimizing Sundowner's Syndrome," 3/15/18 http://www.agingcare.com/Articles/sundowners-syndrome-sadness- agitation-fear-133187.htm

[51] Carol Noren Johnson, "Rain", 11/2/13, http://plantcityladyandfriends.blogspot. com/2013/11/the-rain.html

[52] "Alzheimer's Patients Have Muted Emotions", *The Alzheimer's Reading Room*, http://www.alzheimersreadingroom.com/2010/06/alzheimers-patients-have- muted-emotions.html, used by permission.

Chapter 4

be able to control himself and any control they do have will get worse with the progression of the disease. The caregiver needs to adapt because the patient cannot. It is God's job to be the judge; we are told to obey Scripture but cannot force obedience on the dementia sufferers.[53] Everyone who works with the patient needs the utmost patience. Remember even the care receiver feels overwhelmed and judged.

Anxiety and Confusion

One of the chief reasons that caregivers are needed with dementia patients, is that the care receiver has lost the understanding of his/her surroundings and the events that are happening. Notes, white boards and routines help the patients adjust. They have to be told what is happening.

As the disease progresses, the care receiver needs verbal reminders. *This is your friend here for a visit and we are going to go on a walk together. I am so glad to see you. When our walk is done, we will come right back here.* Distraction of conversation and activities can help. The caregivers need the training because other than establishing routines, the care receivers cannot be trained.

Hallucination, Delusion or Delirium?

Reality can give way to unreality. The caregiver will get little clues from the patient who may even boldly say *"my reality is not your reality"* as my husband once said to me. He may be living at an earlier time period in life and feel that where he is living is not his home. He may not recognize his own family members, or need to be reminded who they are. He may call someone the wrong name. She may think that someone is in the room that is not there. A mirror in the room might show someone not recognizable (themselves) because they are living at another time. While this reality is not correct, the illusion may even be

---

[53] James 4:11, 12

caused by medications. Some of this behavior the caregiver goes along with and some is ignored.

According to *The 36-Hour Day*, **hallucinations** are sensory experiences that are real to the person having them but that others do not have.[54] Drugs can cause hallucinations and so can dementia. The caregiver just has to act calmly about a hallucination and expect them at any time. Perhaps the caregiver says, *How nice that you got a visit from your friend today.* Try to see things from their viewpoint and make comments that reflect their reality. If they see someone in the room that you don't see, ask about that person. Then open the door, thank the person for being there, and then ask that person to leave because you are here now.

> *The discretion of a man makes him slow to anger,*
> *And his glory is to overlook a transgression.*
> Prov. 19:11

Delusions, on the other hand, are not senses, but ideas. "untrue ideas unshakably held by one person."[55] Various strategies can be used to deal with the delusions including redirecting the patient or just concurring with what is said.

Delirium begins suddenly and is dangerous and needs immediate medical treatment. The care receiver is confused and unable to function.

> One important distinguishing feature between dementia and delirium is that delirium usually begins suddenly while dementia develops gradually over months or years. Other symptoms of delirium may include misinterpretation of reality, false ideas, or hallucinations; incoherent speech; sleepiness in the daytime or wakefulness at night; and increased or decreased physical

---

[54] Mace and Rabins, *op. cit.*, p. 136.
[55] Ibid., p. 161

Chapter 4

(motor) activity. Symptoms of delirium tend to vary through the day.[56]

Delirium can accompany Urinary Tract Infections, so it is so important to get treatment for the UTI immediately. Several times I just went to my husband's doctor who trusted my judgment that Herb needed an antibiotic.

Socializing

Care receivers need to socialize as long as possible. At times they will embarrass the caregiver, who may be caught in a situation where others can be offended. Strategies can include distraction or explaining discretely to others around that the loved one has dementia. If the socializing turns to embarrassing sexual behavior, remain calm and get the care receiver to a new area where you can supervise the care receiver. Put your arms under their arm and direct them to a new spot as you distract them. Then run interference and explain the behavior to someone that might have been offended. Remember the Scripture that says that love *does not behave rudely, does not seek its own, is not provoked, thinks no evil.*[57] Often in early stages an Alzheimer's patient will say what he/she thinks!

Wandering

Because the patient may not feel at home where they are (even though they are home), they may decide it is time to go find home.[58] Or, they can be in the car waiting for a quick errand that needs to be performed and decide to get out and shop. This

---

[56] Ibid., p. 289
[57] I Cor. 13:5
[58] Graham, Laurie, "Why do people with dementia wander?", 7/4/15. .http://www. telegraph.co.uk/lifestyle/11717084/Why-do-people-with-dementia-wander. html

happened to my friend Sally who wrote about her husband Jake's wandering:

> Our dog needed her toenails trimmed at the dog groomer. That was a quick fix. Now on to the jewelers to take Jake's watch in for repairs. Jake had left it on the shower ledge and it had moisture on its face. The jeweler was the answer to avoid the watch stopping and rusting.
>
> I parked directly in front of the jewelry store, rolled down the car windows and told Jake to stay in the car with our dog. I would be returning momentarily.
>
> However, when I returned to the car, there was no Jake and our dog was barking. **Panic set in!** Where did my husband go? I hadn't been gone but a moment.
>
> I carried the dog and the two of us set off to find him. Not in a Dollar Store. Not in a laundry. Was he searching for me or for a men's room?
>
> Finally the barbershop. Jake was contently sitting in a barber chair getting his hair cut. I pretended that this was planned and waited until he finished. He did need the haircut after all. I had the money to pay for it--he didn't.
>
> I next dropped him off at the Senior Center and shared this episode with the 2 pm Alzheimer's Association Support group.
>
> Lesson learned: Don't leave my husband in the car alone ever! Do not trust the care of our dog to Jake. And, I am going to start searching for

Chapter 4

a GPS system to track Jake. He no longer uses a cell phone, although he does have an Alzheimer's bracelet.[59]

Soon it becomes apparent that their reasoning is gone and that they need constant supervision. It's three years later and Jake gets out of the passenger seat while Sally is stopped at a fast-foot drive through and Jake's family is considering putting him in an Alzheimer's unit.

I had the fortune (or unfortunate since I broke both ankles falling backward at a drainage ditch) to live as a patient at Huntsville Health and Rehab facility for almost three weeks, observing first hand obvious dementia patients who lived among other residents. One Sunday night I wheeled myself to my friend Virginia's room; this sharp late-ninety- year-old and I both went to the same church. Virginia and I in our wheel chairs started singing hymns and soon other women joined us. Enter "Harriet", not her real name. Harriet lays down on Virginia's bed! Since it was 8:30 p m and I would soon be going to sleep, I dismissed myself and rolled down the hall in my wheel chair to tell a nurse at the north station that Harriet was in my friend's bed. I began wheeling myself back to my bedroom. But the wanderer Harriet was following me. I stopped at my south nurses' station and observed Harriet go down my hall. She was looking for her home, her bed. She even tried to leave the building and set off the alarm. Finally the staff called the north station and someone came to get Harriet and take her home to her room.

Driving

Driving a vehicle takes complex skill and judgment. Observe how they drive when you are a passenger. At some point the care receiver needs to give up driving altogether. This decision to

---

[59] Sally, "Finding Wandering Jake", 5/18/15, http://plantcityladyandfriends.blogspot.com/2015/05/guest-post-finding-wandering-jake.html?m=1, used by permission.

stop driving can be aided by someone outside of the family—the doctor or perhaps the pastor. In the early stages the driver can use a GPS to find his/her way around. However, the person at some point cannot use that instrument. Driving can take wandering to situations where the loved one is in danger. Their driving is eventually not safe.[60] Here are some signs Chris Lliades, M. D., says to watch for:

Needing more help with directions.
Forgetting destinations or where the car was parked.
Having trouble making turns or being
confused by traflc signals.
Receiving citations for moving violations
Putting dents in the car that can't be explained.[61]

For three years after the diagnosis, I struggled and agonized about my husband's driving when we both had two cars. My car wouldn't start one morning while I was to go substitute teach and my husband was already at his work. My neighbor drives me to the school where I was substituting. A new battery is needed. When I call my mechanic, he said that he didn't have a battery for my car—we would need to purchase a battery at the dealership. I called the dealership and told them that my husband would be in to purchase that battery.

A task that would be no problem in the past for my husband becomes a tortured explanation by cell phone to direct him to the dealer after his work. Two wrong turns. A swearing husband. Not a routine trip for my husband who functions fine driving to work and driving back home. I stayed on my cell phone while

---

[60] "Dealing with the Driving Dilemma", *The Alzheimer's Site.com*, n.d.http://blog.thealzheimerssite.com/dealing-with-the-driving-dilema/?utm_source=social&utm_medium=alzaware&utm_campaign=dealing-with-the-driving-dilema&utm_term=20141228#3XxvbiQAzCEgf ILQ.32

[61] Lliades, Crist, "Alzheimer's Disease and Driving Ability", n. d. http://www.everydayhealth.com/alzheimers/alzheimers-disease-and-driving.aspx

Chapter 4

directing him. Mind you I'm in a classroom and hoping silent students don't hear the curse words of my husband at the other end of the cell phone and that they keep working on their tests. (Usually I never talk on a cell phone in the classroom.)

Mission finally accomplished with the purchase of a battery. It would be too difficult to describe to him how he would get to the school where I was teaching and then he would have a wait in the cold. So I told him to just go home and find map directions to the school where I was teaching out on the kitchen counter. Successfully he gets himself home—enough clues in his memory to do that without me.

Time came for him to come pick me up. Students listen while I patiently explain to my husband how to come to the school—the written directions just wouldn't do. He gets to the school and doesn't see me, calling me in the classroom. I tell him to park and wait for school to be dismissed. Every torturous step needed to be described simply to him. After the dismissal bell I find him and we go home. He has been thoroughly upset by the stress of stepping out of his comfort zone while trying to be the gentleman and rescue his wife.

We get home and he prepares to change the battery. I knew I would be in for more swear words as he doesn't do mechanical stuff much anymore and I never did. (That's why we have AAA.)

Meanwhile, coincidentally the plumber Tom calls and asks if he can come by with a plumbing part for the kitchen. "Yes, Tom," I say, "and would you mind very much installing a battery!" It was his pleasure to do that, he says.

When my sweetheart drove, he often got angry at other drivers. Dementia has made him especially impatient and I have had to adjust to his impatience. He remembers to get gas, but that is about all. I have taken over normal maintenance of his car--the oil checks need to be every week because the car is old.

A year after being first diagnosed with dementia, my husband gets a GPS, that we name "Miss Garmin." I program Miss Garmin so he can get home as well as other places. When he leaves the house, he says "Okay, where am I going again?" He calls on the way and asks what is he doing.

"Practice run, sweetheart," I say. He comes back to the house and we try it again. It works this time! He makes it to downtown Plant City and home again quite proud of himself. He loves this device.

Three days later I will be gone all day and not able to mail a book at the post office. I arrange for him to do this. He had forgotten when I called at noon. He is able to make it to the post office and back home. This time he only has to call my cell once.

One day the lawn repair shop calls while I am gone. It is complicated to get there and back. My sweetheart hitches up the trailer and uses "Miss Garmin" to go get the lawn mower and return home. I call him during the day and he doesn't mention that he has retrieved the riding lawn mower. When I return home the front lawn has been mowed!

Nine months later it is a different story. His diagnosis has been given—mixed dementia (Vascular Dementia and Alzheimer's). The next day I cry an ocean of tears on my way home from substitute teaching! I think about how sweet and loving my husband is. I put my glasses on when I came in the door so he wouldn't see I had been crying and gave him a big smile--so glad to see him. I guess I had been hoping for Vascular Dementia instead of Alzheimer's, but not both. My husband was told point blank that he can't drive until he is tested. An appointment is now set to assess his driving skills. He is mad about this. "Of course, I can drive," he says. I reminded him about being sued for our home if he were in an accident because of his Mixed Dementias, and this reasoning didn't make sense to him. Usually he doesn't drive when I am gone anyway--just when we do things together. Several days later in the middle of the night I get his car key out of his jeans.

A month and a half later we talk about his driving test tomorrow. "I will sue if they don't let me drive", he says. Meanwhile my husband vacuums, cleans the carpet and mows the grass. He has his same humor. At a restaurant he blows the

Chapter 4

paper cover off the straw at me as he prepares to drink his ice tea. He prays beautiful prayers, or the simple table grace prayer that I can recite from memory. Of course he feels normal. He has a loving wife and an affectionate dog and a roof over his head. Of course he thinks he can drive.

Rebellion. He apparently went down to Block Buster Video recently and bought some 99-cent movies that I added to his list of movies--not good choices, but he felt free to buy them with the little cash he carries in his wallet. He wasn't supposed to drive until we know the results of that test and the note in his car says that.

One day I get sick to my stomach and need him to drive even though he is not supposed to. He is instructed to bring my purse with my cell phone. I use my cell phone to get the number to the pet groomers so he could call to see if our dog was ready at the groomers.

The front door closes as I hear my husband say he was taking his car to get our dog. Soon he is back in the house looking for the global navigational device plugged into his computer. He finds the address on the Garmin GNP, punches it in and goes to rescue our dog while I am languishing sick at home. When they return, I find my husband trying to put his cell phone into the GPS chord by his computer. I remind him that his cell phone recharger is in our bedroom and that "Miss Garmin" needs to be plugged in at his computer.

The day comes we go to the MaDonna Ptak Center for Alzheimer's and Memory Loss/Memory Disorders Clinic at the Morton Plant Neuroscience Clinic in Clearwater, Florida. In the morning my husband takes the DriveABLE Road Evaluation test which is *not sufficient to resolve driver competency. The DriveABLE Road Evaluation is needed to determine driver competence.*

That afternoon my husband takes his road test at the Suncoast Safety Council also in Clearwater. I believe he passed it, but you never know what the neurologist, Dr. Raj, will say. We have yet to meet him, but he is the professional who gave us the Mixed

Dementia diagnosis (two kinds of dementia) at the USF Byrd Alzheimer's Research Institute in Tampa.

Four days later we get the word by phone at home and I get the word on my cell. Officially he passes both tests and can drive! One happy husband who, mind you, would have sued if he couldn't drive!

One Sunday we are on our way home from church and are hit by a DUI driver. I am driving and that car is totaled. Both of us have physical therapy, and husband recognizes that we no longer need two cars.

Three years after the general diagnosis of dementia, there is one more driving test that he passed pending a six-month review. We attend a memorial service where I spoke in behalf of a dear friend Sandy who had prayed daily for my caregiver journey, while losing her battle to Muscular Dystrophy. On the way back, my husband out of the blue says,

I will be so glad when I don't drive anymore.
I desire to be a passenger.

For me it was incredible that he makes this decision and also that he remembers he made it.

"You may not drive" are hard words for anyone. These behaviors are different for everyone with the disease and wisdom is needed to handle them. The caregiver needs to share with trusted others how difficult this is—perhaps joining an Alzheimer's Association Support Group that meets once a month and/or having other support within the church.

CHAPTER 5
CAREGIVING STRESS

With all of these problem behaviors that manifest themselves in the loved one comes significant stress for the caregiver.

Just when one behavior gets managed, another behavior comes along. The result is stress for the caregiver who doesn't always want to admit that they cannot handle stress. They want to protect the reputation of the care receiver and manage things themselves—take care of their own. Scripture has many cries for help.

> *Save me, O God, for the waters are up to my neck.*
> *I sink in deep mire,*
> *Where there is no standing;*
> *I have come into deep waters.*
> *Where the floods overflow me.*
> *I am weary with my crying;*
> *My throat is dry;*
> *My eyes fail while I wait for my God.* [62]

The closer relationship the caregiver has to the care receiver, the more stress he or she will feel as the disease progresses.

---

[62] Psalm 69:1-3

Financial Stress

This includes financial stress and even planning for retirement may not cover the cost.[63] Often then the caregiver doesn't assess what the finances will be like once the care receiver has passed away and there is less income. Some solutions early on such as a second mortgage may come back to bite the family after the death of the care receiver. When the home is then sold in a short sale, and that second mortgage is forgiven, the Internal Revenue Service may come back to demand taxes from that second mortgage "income" being forgiven. Planning ahead of time for those contingencies could alleviate some of the stress. Even if the caregiver has made sure the loved one is safe, has not ignored the disease and has established good routines, the responsibility of caregiving is not complete! One more thing needs to happen— taking care of one's own stress that comes to the caregiver who is trying to keep the loved one calm. The tension never lets up. Dr. Ruth Westheimer at 84 years of age writes: "It must be acknowledged that the challenges facing caregivers who are dealing with Alzheimer's disease are enormous. If you are responsible for taking care of someone with Alzheimer's, especially in the advanced stages, you have quite a weight on your shoulders."[64]

The Alzheimer's Association offers a booklet, *Take Care of Yourself: Ten Ways to be a Healthier Caregiver* and gives these ten suggestions:

1. Understand what's going on as early as possible.
2. Know what community resources are available.
3. Become an educated caregiver.
4. Get help.

---

[63] http://globalnation.inquirer.net/124409/family-caregivers-in-us-face-emotional-financial-strain-says-study

[64] Westheimer, Dr. Ruth K. with Pierre A. Lehu, Dr. *Ruth's Guide for the Alzheimer's Caregiver: How to Care for Your Loved One without Getting Overwhelmed . . . and without Doing It All Yourself,* (Fresno, CA: Quill Driver Books, 2012), ix, used by permission.

5. Take care of yourself.
6. Manage your level of stress.
7. Accept changes as they occur.
8. Make legal and financial plans.
9. Give yourself credit, not guilt.
10. Visit your doctor regularly.[65]

The same booklet lists these ten symptoms of caregiver stress: denial, anger, social withdrawal, anxiety, depression, exhaustion, sleeplessness, irritability, lack of concentration and health problems.

Furthermore, the caregiver cannot share deep feelings with their loved one unless it is at a beginning stage of dementia when the loved one can actually encourage the caregiver.[66] Depression does not have to be a normal part of aging. However, caregivers, young or old, become depressed. It's constant—repeated questions, dealing with problem behaviors such as anger mentioned in the last chapter, planning nutrition, planning socialization and other outings, making the house Alzheimer's proof, budgeting, noting changes in behavior that might signal an Urinary Tract Infection or worse yet delirium. Blogger Bob DeMarco says dementia caregivers torture themselves and continues "Alzheimer's often robs patients of the ability to say 'yes', so instead they say what comes easiest—No."[67] Too much stress and the caregiver can develop physical illness, thus becoming the patient.[68]

---

[65] *Take Care of Yourself: Ten Ways to be a Healthier Caregiver,* (Alzheimer's Association, 2009.), used by permission.

[66] Carol Noren Johnson, "Shot of Joy," April 26, 2013, Plant *City Lady and Friends Blog, http://plantcityladyandfriends.blogspot.com/2012/04/shot-of-joy.html.*

[67] Bob DeMarco, "Why Do Dementia Caregivers Torture Themselves?" October 15, 2013, https://www.alzheimersreadingroom.com/2012/03/why-do-alzheimers- caregivers-torture.html, used by permission.

[68] Bob DeMarco, "The Alzheimer's Caregiver Can Become the Patient," June 25, 2013, *Alzheimer's Reading Room Blog, https://www. alzheimersreadingroom. com/2009/01/alzheimers-caregiver-can-become-patient.html,* used by permission.

Hero Stress and Chronic Negative Stress

The caregiver steps up to the plate and does it all, it appears to others. Being the hero becomes tiring, and eventually the caregiver can break down. Depression sets in and the rate of death for caregivers is higher than non-caregivers. The Alzheimer's Reading Room reports:

> According to the Alzheimer's Association, more than 80% of Alzheimer's caregivers report that they frequently experience high levels of stress, and nearly half say they suffer from depression. It's not difficult to see why. The national Family Caregiver Alliance terms caregiver depression "one of today's all-too-silent health crises." The alliance estimates that caregiving spouses between the ages of 66 and 96 who are experiencing mental or emotional strain have a 63% higher risk of dying than people the same age who are not caregivers.[69]

Acute stress is also called flight-or-fright stress. Here the body reacts immediately to a threat.[70] Chronic stress means continuing stress where the body doesn't have time to recover.[71] Chronic stress is what a caregiver experiences day in and day out. Eustress is not the absence of stress, but positive stress, or **hero stress,** that keeps us challenged and keeps us away from getting depressed.[72] Tears can instruct us. Christian blogger Emily Freeman advises that we listen to our tears.

---

[69] Ibid.
[70] Scott, Elizabeth, "FindEffectiveStressReliefTechnuquesforDifferent TypesofStress", 4/3/18 http://stress.about.com/od/stressmanagement glossary/g/accutestress.htm
[71] Scott, Elizabeth, "What Is Chronic Stress?", 2/14/18 http://stress.about.com/ od/stressmanagementglossary/g/Chronicstress.htm
[72] Scott, Elizabeth, "Why Eustress Is Your Friend", 6/14/18 http://stress.about.com/ od/stressmanagementglossary/g/Eustress.htm

Chapter 5

> When was the last time you felt the stinging gift in your own eyes, this most natural reminder that you are alive, here, human?
>
> Maybe it's been a while for you. There's nothing wrong with that. But the next time the tears rise up to meet you, don't brush them aside.
>
> Greet them, receive them, and listen for the life they bring.[73]

When tears and stress happen, take heed. There is a message for us. We may have too much chronic stress, or we may have bitterness that we need to confess. If there is too much stress, we can develop physical illnesses. Yes, we are human, but *let us hold fast the confession of our hope without wavering, for He who promised is faithful* (Hebrews 10:23). We just need to hold on and "do the next thing." When she spoke, Elizabeth Elliott often quoted the *Do the Next Thing* Poem, inspiring her audience.[74] That next thing to do helps us capitalize on good stress or the eustress that counteracts the chronic negative stress. Find projects and hobbies to relax. Elisabeth would die from dementia at age 88, but left her legacy often quoted.[75]

Read literature and meditate on Scripture. Connect with friends. Pastor John Piper talks about four duties of 1) joy, 2) rejoicing in God, 3) asking God for the joy to be restored, and with the fourth duty he writes:

---

[73] Freeman, Emily, "One way to Listen for Your Life," November 16, 2013 http:// www.incourage.me/2013/11/one-way-to-listen-for-your-life.html

[74] Colleen Chao, "Do the next thing: Wisdom from Elisabeth Elliot," 6/16/15, https://erlc.com/resource-library/articles/do-the-next-thing-wisdom- from-elisabeth-elliot.

[75] Smith, Tyler, "In Memory of Elisabeth Elliot: 30 of Her Most Inspiring Quotes, 6/15/15. https://blog.logos.com/2015/06/in-memory-of-elisabeth-elliot-30-o f-her-most-inspiring-quotes/.

And the fourth thing we say, when we counsel the depressed Christian to be up and doing something good is, "Be sure to thank God as you work that he has given you at least the will to work." Do not say, "But it is hypocritical to thank God with my tongue when I don't feel thankful in my heart." There is such a thing as hypocritical thanksgiving. Its aim is to conceal ingratitude and get the praise of men. That is not you aim. Your aim in loosing your tongue with words of gratitude is that God would be merciful and fill your *words* with the *emotion* of true gratitude. You are not seeking the praise of men; you are seeing the mercy of God. You are not hiding the hardness of ingratitude, but hoping for the in breaking of the Spirit.[76]

Do the next thing with a joyful spirit that God gives.

Common Caregivers Emotions

Linda Fisher has been a caregiver for her husband and blogs about these caregiver emotions: guilt, resentment, anger, worry, loneliness, defensiveness and grief. I noted that nowhere does she suggest biblical solutions for these emotions.[77] Also, Carol Bradley Bursack writes advice about caregivers apologizing for their outbursts of anger.

> Family members and friends who are clueless about the realities of caregiving often add to the stress by offering "advice," which sounds to you like criticism rather than help. You're a good person and likely they are, too, so 'you stuff your

---

[76] John Piper, *When the Darkness Will Not Lift* (Wheaton, IL: Crossways Books, 2006), pp. 50-51, used by permission.
[77] Linda Fisher, *Early Onset* Blog, *2013* posts on *May* 25, 31, June 8, 15, 22, July 13, 21

> irritation, bite back a sarcastic response and let the comments or actions pass – this time. . . .
>
> One reason we often direct our anger and resentment on those closest to us is that we feel safe. We feel that these people won't abandon us.
>
> We don't intend to treat our friends shabbily. After all, they deserve our loving kindness. Yet, if we don't find a healthy outlet for our anger and resentment over what we feel is undeserved criticism about our caregiving skills, the anger is likely to come out sideways and our best friend takes the hit.
>
> Once you understand why you behaved poorly to your friend, you may be able to offer a sincere apology. Hopefully, you will also have made progress in learning to handle your emotions in a healthier way, so that a person who is your biggest supporter doesn't become your target the next time you blow.[78]

The above is not fully the biblical response. Yes, people are not expected to know what caregiving is like. If we are able to graciously say nothing and pray, that works. If we must say something, choosing our words carefully is the biblical way to proceed: *So then, my beloved brethren, let every man be swift to hear, slow to speak, slow to wrath* (James 1:19). But when we snap back, we need to repent and properly confess our faults to that person and to the LORD.[79]

---

[78] Bursack, Carol Bradley, "Apologizing After Caregiver Burnout Causes a Blowup", 11/16/13, https://www.agingcare.com/Articles/ apologizing-after-caregiver-stress-causes-blowup-159849.htm?utm source= Newsletter& utm medium=Ema i l& utm c a mpa ign=Newsletter+-+November+16%2C+2013, used by permission.

[79] Psalm 32:5; 1 John 1:9

Taking a Break--Respite

The need for respite comes into the picture. Even Christ drew away from the crowds to pray, often going up on a mountain.[80] Deborah Howard writes about the continual "on duty" strain of the tasks of caregivers.

> Being responsible for the well-being of others may place us under a tremendous strain. Caregivers are generally sleep-deprived, exhausted, and easily distracted. They often are "on duty" twenty-four hours a day, seven days a week. With people depending on them, they frequently find themselves with very few moments alone, and even then they may feel that they are "on call."[81]

Carol Bradley Bursack suggests the caregiver get away. Respite needs to be found and she offers suggestions for your planning for the care receiver back home while you are away.[82] There are many ideas for finding respite.

Remember, there's no set formula or protocol when it comes to respite. It's a caregiver's break that's all yours. It may be a phone call with a friend while your loved one naps. Or it might be a weekend away with your spouse. It could be getting a massage or going to the library. The possibilities are as unique as you and your situation – but whatever you do, don't pass up a chance for a change of pace. You need it – and your loved one needs you to have it.[83]

---

[80] Luke 5:15; Matthew 14:23 and Mark 1:35, 36
[81] Howard, Deborah, *Sunsets: Reflections for Life's Final Journey* (Wheaton, IL: Crossway Books, 2005), p. 303.
[82] Bursack, Carol Bradley, "How to Unplug From Caregiving," n. d. https://www.agingcare.com/articles/how-to-unplug-from-caregiving-163043.htm used by permission, used by permission.
[83] Sollitto,Marlo, „"Where to Find Respite", 12/14/17, https://www.agingcare.com/Articles

Chapter 5

My friend Sally has many hobbies and plans time away from Jake with someone to stay with him. I substitute taught some days and my neighbor looked in on Herb. When Sally and I went out to eat with our husbands, we sat side-by-side and chatted with our husbands across the table. Respite, hobbies, and friendships are essential for managing stress.

Support

Besides respite, the caregiver needs much love and support. Kathy Birkett suggests you keep a list for when someone asks what he or she can do to help. She goes on to write:

> Asking for Help is Not Weakness!
>
> One survey reported that, compared to family caregivers who were not spouses, more than half (58%) of spousal caregivers had no outside help from family, friends or paid caregivers. Yikes!
>
> Unfortunately, spousal caregivers seem to tell others that they are doing fine. It is their duty, after all.
>
> Most find the tasks of caregiving slowly overwhelm them as they seem to add up over time, instead of starting out being too much. The tasks seem to pile up before most even realize that they are doing so much and become burned out.[84]

Mittleman, Roth, Clay and Haley confirm that counseling and support help: "Counseling and support hold promise as a means of preserving health among vulnerable dementia caregivers

---

[84] Birkett,, Kathy, "Family Dynamics of Caregiving When a Spouse is Primary Caregiver," n. d. http://seniorcarecorner.com/family-dynamics-spouse-caregiver

who are at risk not only for declining health, but also increased mortality."[85] That caregiver and the patient both need prayer and the caregiver needs someone to listen and help provide a break from the demands of caregiving. Prayer requests early in the disease dare not be mentioned publically in a congregational worship service in the presence of the loved one who wishes to appear normal to others.

Just having someone ask the caregiver these questions can be enormously supportive. Marie Marley on Bob DeMarco's blog gets many comments from caregivers and she writes:

> Many caregivers get abandoned by friends and family. The reasons for this varies widely--ranging from denial, dysfunction, to fear of Alzheimer's. Many times friends and family while living their own busy lives fail to realize what is happening to the caregiver. An Alzheimer's caregiver might vent to me or vent on the Internet about this issue; but, they rarely tell friends and family what they need.[86]

That blog post contains a wealth of ideas.

---

[85] Mary S. Mittleman, David I. Roth, Olivio J. Clay, and William El Haley, "Preserving Health of Alzheimer Caregivers: Impact of a Spouse Caregiver Intervention," September 2007, http://www.researchgate.net/ publication/6035373_Preserving_health_of_Alzheimer_caregivers_impact_of_a_spouse_caregiver_intervention

[86] Bob DeMarco, "Where Are the Alzheimer's Caregiver Helpers?" June 7, 2013, *Alzheimer's Reading Room Blog*, http://www.alzheimersreadingroom.com/2013/06/Alzheimers-Caregiver-Help.html used by permission.

Certainly the local church needs to include caregivers in their ministries. Some churches have Alzheimer's support groups.[87] A caregiver should not have to be a "shut-in twenty-four seven." If Christ needed to get away, so do they. Caregivers need to ask for this relief and support, but how much better if it is offered without having to ask for it. Marie Marley continues:

> Don't allow Alzheimer's to take control of the caregiver—form a team to take control of the problem. The caregiver gets a life, the sufferer gets more effective care, and the team gets the wonderful feeling that comes team with doing something and getting involved.
>
> Note: I realize the above does not apply to all families and friends of Alzheimer's caregivers. On the other hand, I know that this article is about one of life's dirty little secrets.[88]

Family Tensions

Family members can try to manage the patient from a distance and not really understand the situation. Furthermore, the patient may prefer his or her own home and show irritation visiting a relative. The relative may have a hard time accepting that change. Add the dynamic of a stepfamily and caregiver stress can be magnified.

Because the disease is so difficult, the caregiver needs to tolerate that not everyone (family as well as friends) will be able to understand and appreciate the complexity. Christian lawyer

---

[87] Michelle Bearden, "Bernie's War," *The Tampa Tribune*, August 11, 2013, 1,14. Certainly someone in the church can offer to stay with the dementia loved one while the caregiver goes to a counseling appointment, to a support group, or even to church. More on churches in chapter six.

[88] Bob DeMarco, op. cit.

Ken Sande has written a book on making peace with others. Sande brings up the point that old family hurts can play into the current family crisis. For example, Sande was asked by adult brothers and sisters to settle a dispute about where their mother should live. He writes:

> I finally asked to talk with the two sisters in private to help them discuss the personal offenses that were obviously fueling their quarrel. Putting the guardianship issue aside for a moment, I helped them to examine their attitudes and behavior toward each other. As we studied a few relevant Bible passages, the Lord began to work in their hearts. After about thirty minutes, the real cause of the conflict finally came to the surface.
>
> Almost twenty years earlier, one of the women had said something that deeply hurt the other one. The offended sister had tried to pretend that she was not hurt, but she could not help brooding over the insult, and their relationship was steadily poisoned. Consequently, they opposed each other in everything, even if it involved their mother's care.
>
> As we continued to talk about their relationship, they began to deal honestly with their feelings and actions. They saw how they had been dishonoring God and hurting other people. As God opened their hearts, they confessed their sins and forgave each other. With tears in their eyes, they embraced each other for the first time in twenty years. They soon joined their brothers and sister and explained what had happened. Within five minutes, all seven children agreed that their mother would be happier in her own home, and in another fifteen

minutes they negotiated a schedule for her care. As you can image, when they told her the news that evening, the reconciliation of her children brought her even more joy than the decision about her living arrangement.[89]

The tension had everything to do with continuing tension between two sisters, but the solution was a spiritual one. That family stress can even manifest after the loved one dies; a family member may feel guilty that he or she has not been there during the illness and lash out at the caregiver who has been holding it together for years.

Other Suggestions

Luminita Saviuc, "The Purpose Fairy", has written a blog post "15 Things You Should Give Up To Be Happy".[90] *Happiness* however is not a biblical term, but *joy* is a biblical term and Christ promised us peace and joy amidst our suffering. Caregivers can live so that one day, like the parable of the talents, they will hear, *Well done, thou good and faithful servant; you were faithful over a few things . . . Enter into the joy of your lord.*[91] There are things one can do to be joyful in the caregiving journey as mentioned in my Plant City Lady and Friends Blog post.[92] The fifteen items from Saviuc's blog are in italics with my new comments and Scripture added.

---

[89] Sande, Ken, *The Peacemaker: A Biblical Guide to Resolving Personal Conflict*, 2nd ed. (Grand Rapids, Michigan: Baker Books, 1997) 23-24, used by permission.

[90] Luminita D. Saviuc, "15 Things You Should Give Up To Be Happy," updated May 30, 2011, https://www.purposefairy.com/3308/15-things-you-should-give- up-in-order-to-be-happy/, used by permission.

[91] Matthew 25:21.

[92] Carol Noren Johnson, "15 Things Caregivers Can Do to Be Joyful," August 10, 2012, *Plant City Lady and Friends Blog,* http://plantcityladyandfriends.blogspot. com/2012/08/15-things-caregivers-can-do-to-be-joyful.html

1. *"Give up your need to be right."* As explained in chapter three the brain of the loved one is changing, and the caregiver needs to adapt.

2. *"Give up your need to control."* A wife will need to be the best helpmate, but she cannot run the household as she was once able to do. Tom and Karen Brenner write on the *Alzheimer's Reading Room Blog*: "You are learning in this caregiving journey the very important lesson that all of us must learn: You know that we can't control or influence everything in our world. Those things we can't control or influence, we simply have to LET IT BE!"[93]

3. *"Give up blame."* Christ was asked whom to blame--blind man or his parents for that blind man's condition. Christ answered that neither sinned but that the purpose was, according to John 9:3, *that the works of God should be revealed in him*. There is no one to blame for the Alzheimer's and certainly not God.

4. *"Give up your self-defeating talk."* Philippians 4:8 reads *Whatever things are true, whatever things are noble, whatever things are just, whatever things are pure, whatever things are lovely, whatever things are of good report, if there is any virtue and if there is anything praiseworthy—meditate on these things.*

5. *"Give up your limiting beliefs."* Philippians 4:13 encourages *I can do all things through Christ who strengthens me.*

6. *"Give up complaining."* See Philippians 2:14; Prov. 29:11; 19:11.

---

[93] Tom and Karen Brenner, "Let It Be, Let It Go", January 25, 2013, *Alzheimer's Reading Room Blog*, http://www.alzheimersreadingroom.com/2012/03/let-it-be- let-it-go.html, used by permission.

7. *"Give up the luxury of criticism."* The care receiver's world is changing, but not their need for unconditional love. Proverbs 19:11 reads *The discretion of a man makes him slow to anger, and his glory is to overlook a transgression.*

8. *"Give up your need to impress others."* 1 John 2:16 reads *For all that is in the world—the lust of the flesh, the lust of the eyes, and the pride of life—is not of the Father but is of the world.*

9. *"Give up your resistance to change."* Proverbs 19:21 reads *There are many plans in a man's heart, nevertheless the LORD's counsel— that will stand.*

10. *"Give up labels."* The care receiver is a person, not a diagnosis. The Brenners write "We cannot make them stop pitying us. We cannot make them stop feeling afraid, or uncomfortable. It is hard enough to control these feelings in ourselves. We cannot hope to try and control these negative feelings in other people. We just have to let it be. While you cannot change the condition of dementia, you can change how you look at it, how you live with it.[94]

11. *"Give up your fears."* 1 Peter 5:7 reads *casting all your care upon Him, for He cares for you.*

12. *"Give up your excuses."* 1 Peter 5:6 reads *humble yourselves under the mighty hand of God.*

13. *"Give up the past."* Philippians 3:13-14 reads *forgetting those things which are behind and reaching forward to those things which are ahead, I press toward the goal for the prize of the upward call of God in Christ Jesus.*

14. *"Give up attachments."* Hebrews 13:5 reads *Let your conduct be without covetousness; be content with such things as you*

---

[94] Ibid.

have. For He Himself has said, "I will never leave you nor forsake you."

15. "Give up living your life to other people's expectations." Proverbs 29:25 reads *The fear of man brings a snare, but whoever trusts in the LORD shall be safe.*

Add the joy of discipleship. We read in James 1:2-3: *Count it all joy when you fall into various trials, knowing that the testing of your faith produces patience. But let patience have its perfect work, that you may be perfect and complete, lacking nothing.* Joy is a byproduct of discipleship. Christ said to his disciples, *Take My yoke upon you and learn from Me, for I am gentle and lowly in heart, and you will find rest for your souls. For My yoke is easy and My burden is light.*[95] We can have joy in trials because those trials are working out the LORD's perfect work and we are becoming a disciple.

One day I swallowed my husband's pills, and my discipleship was severely tested. I had to go to the hospital. I did not need his diabetic, heart and Alzheimer's medicine. I started to feel poorly. My husband's pills for Tuesday were missing but I hadn't taken my pills. I had my husband call 911. Fortunately, my husband was able to stay with his daughter while I was in the hospital. I was so grateful for that step-daughter and also for her brother who kept my husband the week I was on a cruise.

Dealing With the Stress

Don't just give up those fifteen items. Add more strategies. Add eustress if you will, to fight acute and chronic stress and depression. Have prayerful goals each day to fight depression. Develop your own caregiving strategy such as:

1. Keep on while
2. Cutting back while
3. Doing the next thing while

---

[95] Matthew 11:29-30

Chapter 5

4. Keeping a journal while
5. Having verses and hymns to focus on while
6. Reminding yourself that God loves you and will be with you while
7. Getting wise counsel and
8. Finding something fun to do.

Develop a Scripture verse or passage fund to meditate on when challenged with stress and depression. Perhaps find a hymn such as "Great Is Thy Faithfulness" and sing it over and over silently or out loud. His yoke is easy.

D. Martyn Lloyd-Jones in his book, *Spiritual Depression: Its Causes and Cure*, points out that "one of the greatest problems in our life in this world, not only for Christians, but for all people, is the right handling of our feelings and emotions."[96] He points out that so much of the epistles are about the tyranny of circumstances or the things that happen to us. He heralds Philippians 4:6-7 as *undoubtedly one of the noblest, greatest and most comforting statements which is to be found anywhere in any extant literature.*[97] These verses say:

> Be anxious for nothing, but in everything by prayer and, with thanksgiving, let your requests be made known to God; and the peace of God, which surpasses all understanding, will guard your hearts and minds through Christ Jesus.

Lloyd-Jones writes earlier in the book about faith.

> A Christian is not meant to be dejected when everything goes wrong. He is told to 'rejoice'. Feelings belong to happiness alone, rejoicing takes

---

[96] Lloyd-Jones, D. Martyn, *Spiritual Depression: Its Causes and Cure* (Grand Rapids, Michigan: Wm. B. Eerdmans Publishing Co., 1965), p.109, used by permission.
[97] Ibid., p. 261.

in something much bigger than feelings; and if faith were a matter of feelings only, then when things go wrong and feeling change, faith will go. But faith is not a matter of feelings only; faith takes up the whole man including his mind, his intellect and his understanding.[98]

Christ told the multitudes, *whoever does not bear his cross and come after Me cannot be My disciple.*[99] Yet caregiving can often be a 36 hour day.[100]

Taking up the cross of caregiving makes one a disciple, not a martyr.

It is faith, not feelings, that makes one a disciple.

> *I called on the LORD in distress;*
> *The LORD answered me*
> *And set me in a broad place.*
> *The LORD is on my side;*
> *I will not fear.*
> *What can man do to me?*
> *The LORD is for me among*
> *Those who help me;*
> *Therefore I shall see my desire*
> *On those who hate me.*
> *It is better to trust in the LORD*
> *Than to put confidence in man.*
> *It is better to trust in the LORD*
> *Than to put confidence in princes.*
> Psalm 118:5-9

---

[98] Ibid, p. 142.
[99] Luke 14:27.
[100] Mace, Nancy and Peter Rabins, op. cit.

Chapter 5

Caregiving does demand that we *be as wise as serpents and harmless as doves.*[101] Unlike other professions, caregivers will get their rewards in heaven, not here on earth.

Take heed that you do not do your charitable deeds before men, to be seen by them. Otherwise you have no reward from your Father in heaven.[102]

---

[101] Matthew 10:16
[102] Matthew 6:1

CHAPTER 6

LOVING THE CARE RECEIVER

*You shall rise before the gray headed
and honor the presence of an old man,
and fear your God:
I am the LORD.*
Leviticus 19:31

I realized that how I lived my life loving my husband with dementia might have an impact on others. Caregiver Jay Echternach also did. He writes in a blog post on Eternal Perspective Ministries how holding hands with his care receiver wife is so important:

> Now it is the ONLY thing we can share consistently. From the comment I walk in, no words are spoken and she rarely if even says my name (unless to our daughter Jennifer). Her eyes finally noticed me and she reaches out her good right hand and holds my hand tightly for the next hour. Her fingers don't stroke, her hand doesn't twist or turn; just a firm, hard grip that NEVER lets go.

Chapter 6

So much is said between us in a relatively simple act. The need or desire to be close and know you is safe. The tactile sense of touch and being ever closer to her and the feeling of shared experience. A physical act that confirms we are still together in body, mind, and spirit. It is a priceless act that words cannot describe.

We shared a moment this part December that I will never forget. She had been experiencing fits of tears and terrible emotion in her face that spoke of pain, fear, or whatever was ailing her, unable to share or speak what was hurting her. I tried for almost 30 minutes to change her mood; laughing, telling stories, feeding her, HOLDING HER HAND—but nothing worked. She cried all the more, searching my eyes for a cure that was not coming.

My heart finally broke and I fell on my knees, gripping both her hands and burring my face in her lap, unable to watch her cry any longer. I sobbed audibly and all I could say was, "I'm sorry, so sorry!" Sorry I can't help, sorry for anything I had ever done to cause you pain, sorry we are separated by a disease that cannot be healed.

God and His angels must have heard my prayer. Within seconds she let go of my hands and cupper my face with her good hand, pulled it up ever so slightly, looked deeply into my eyes, and said "It's going to be alright!" Immediately she stopped crying and sat there staring out beyond me without a care in the world.

> There was no oxygen in my lungs to breathe. Tears streamed down my face, I pressed my cheek to hers and kissed her softly.
>
> Human touch heals a broken heart and speaks a thousand words without an utterance. It's a touch we have shared for over 42 years but never like this or more tender. [103]

Like this gentleman, I was so glad that I could love my husband and be there for him the rest of his days and now encourage others on the same stressful journey.

Tom and Karen Brenner have positive suggestions beyond the agony of caregiving stress. They write: *The magical mystery tour of dementia is all new territory, and it is different for each person. You will have to decide how you are going to take this journey, but you should know that you are never alone, no matter how wild the ride, how frightening the road.*[104] Sally and I appreciated all the socializations that happened for Jake and Herb. Caregiving is not an inconvenience. It is a way of loving as we are all called to do in the body of Christ. *Still Alice* is a novel by neuroscientist Lisa Genova about a professor who suffers from Early Onset Alzheimer's. The fictional Dr. Alice Howland says some important things about her disease in a speech she read to a Dementia Care Conference:

> Please don't look at our scarlet A's and write us off. Look us in the eye, talk directly to us. Don't panic or take it personally if we make mistakes, because we will. We will repeat ourselves, we will misplace things, and we will get lost. We will

---

[103] Echternach, Jay, "Human Touch. . ." https://www.epm.org/blog/2018/Feb/7/human-touch-heals-and-connects-even-through-alzhei used by permission.

[104] Brenner, Tom and Karen, *You Say Goodbye and We Say Hello: The Montessori Method for Positive Dementia Czre*, (Chicago: Brennerpathways.org, 2012), p. 16, used by permission.

Chapter 6

> forget your name and what you said two minutes ago. We will also try our hardest to compensate for and overcome our cognitive losses....
>
> My yesterdays are disappearing, and my tomorrows are uncertain, so what I do I live for? I live for each day. I live in the moment. Some tomorrow soon, I'll forget that I stood before you and gave this speech. But just because I'll forget it some tomorrow doesn't mean that I didn't live every second of it today. I will forget today, but that doesn't mean that today didn't matter.[105]

At the end of the book the Alzheimer's sufferer is asked by her actress daughter *what do you feel?* Alice responds *I feel love. It's about love.*

> The actress squealed, rushed over to Alice, kissed her on the cheek, and smiles, every crease of her face delighted.
>
> "Did I get it right?" asked Alice.
>
> "You did, Mom. You got it exactly right."[106]

Memory doesn't continue, but emotions do. Scientists have theories about the emotions in the brain that helps explain dementia.[107] Certified Geriatric Care Manager Carole Larkin goes on to explain:

> But with Alzheimer's and some of the other diseases, the portions of our brains that are

---
[105] Genova, Lisa, *Still Alice* (Waterville, Maine: Wheeler Publishing, large print edition, 2009), pp 346-347.
[106] Ibid., p. 397.
[107] https://www.alzheimersreadingroom.com/2013/08/the-logic-behind-alzheimers- fear-and.html . Used by permission.

involved in logic can and do become more damaged than the portions of our brains involved in emotions.

In addition, the "filter" in our brains, (the part that allows you to think one thing, but say something else that is softer, gentler, and more socially acceptable), gets damaged pretty early in Alzheimer's. Comments and behaviors that persons with Alzheimer's show to us all the time confirm this idea.

The Bible contrasts agape love and brotherly love. 1 Corinthians 13:12-13 says about agape love: *For now we see in a mirror dimly, but then face to face. Now I know in part, but then I shall know just as I also am known. And now abide faith, hope, love, and these three; but the greatest of these is love.*

We are commanded to love the LORD and others in Scripture, as Christ has loved us (John 13:35). Our love is to suffer long (1 Corinthians 13:4). How can this be with the difficult season of caregiving? 2 Peter 1:3-7 tells us that we are given everything that *pertains to life and godliness*. At times caregiving will be love that doesn't expose the problems of our care receivers to others as in Proverbs 10:12 and I Peter 4:8.

Looking Out for the Interests of the Care Receiver

We are commanded to be holy in 1 Peter 1:16, and out of holiness comes as the most important fruit of the spirit which is love; according to Galatians 5:14 love fulfills the law and 1 Corinthians 13:13 says *the greatest of these is love*. Being an Alzheimer's caregiver means selflessly looking out for the interest of another. This requires self-discipline in the caregiver. He needs to not only look out for his own household and family, but also the concerns of the person in his charge. Sometimes this means that the caregiver takes responsibility for his own health so that he will be able to be there for his loved one. The caregiver needs to take one day at a time and yet he is to look down the road to future situations in the journey. You cannot control aspects of the disease, but you can control your own behavior, become disciplined and obey God's Word.

Be Willing to Give Up Earthly Treasures

Some caregivers may need to quit work to take care of their loved one. *Do not lay up for yourselves treasures on earth, where moth and rust destroy and where thieves break in and steal; but lay up for yourselves treasures in heaven, where neither moth nor rust destroys and where thieves do not break in and steal. For where your treasure is, there your heart will be also* (Matthew 6:19-21). Giving up treasures include not being able to work because you are a caregiver, cashing in possessions to keep within the budget, and foregoing vacations and luxuries. Families may or may not come to caregiver's rescue financially. Caregivers often write about bitterness but will have to avoid that bitter spirit (Hebrews 12:15).

It is not only important to give up hopes of wealth, but also to give up possessions, to simplify. *The Complete Guide to Alzheimer's Proofing Your Home* and others books can help the caregiver.[108]

Be Willing to Give Up Rights

Christ gave up His position in heaven, even washed the feet of his disciples. Bear fruit *keeping with repentance,* we read in Matthew 3:8. John the Baptist called people to repentance because Christ would be coming. In a parallel passage in Luke 3:8 John tells his followers not to rely on being in Abraham's lineage, because Christ can (and is) raising up new people as it were from stones. Repentance is a biblical concept and in caregiving, so much adjustment and change are needed that one is constantly repenting and changing directions as one accepts

---

[108] Warner, Mark L *The Complete Guide to Alzheimer's Proofing Your Home* (West Lafayette, IN: Purdue University Press, 2000).

being a caregiver. It is not sinful to have to adapt, but adapting with a root of bitterness is sinful and should be repented of. You have to learn to speak what is necessary, to say one concept at a time and to repeat it as needed. This means a radical shift in how to talk with our loved one. We have to learn to speak Alzheimer's as well as give up rights.

If you feel entitled to an easy life where everything is fair, that your loved one stays the same, it is not going to happen when you are a caregiver, or, for that matter, with many other kinds of suffering in our world after the fall. Dr. John Zeisel in his helpful book, *I'm Still Here*, says "It is kinder and much more respectful to understand the respond to whatever reality the other expresses. It also reduced anxiety and aggression and is therefore a successful form of treatment."[109] I have to give up my rights to an easy life perhaps for a manicured lawn.

Live In the Moment and Be With Your Loved One

Christ told his followers to not worry and to seek first His kingdom in Luke 12. The more you are with your loved one, the more they will recognize you as kin. One day Jake asked his wife Sally where his wife was and she told him "Your wife loves you very much." At other times Jake recognizes Sally as his wife and they tell each other they love each other. Recently Sally and Jake moved into a Christian retirement community, that does have a wing for him when his Alzheimer's gets worse—such a proactive move. Because Sally has been there for Jake all along, this move has been successful. I commend Sally for bravely making that move. Their same living room and bedroom furniture make Jake feel right at home with Sally. Amenities include a safe shower and guardrails. Jake noticed a picture of the friends Carol and Herb that he loves. Sally and I communicate each day even though I live in another state now. When dementia touches you, you love all concerned.

---

[109] Zeisel, John, *I'm Still Here: A New Philosophy of Alzheimer's Care*, (New York: The Penguin Group) p. 156.

Chapter 6

Learn How to Talk to Someone Who Has Alzheimer's

Get right in front of the dementia person and look them in the eyes. Do not exhibit hostile body language that says *what do you need now?* One has to learn how to speak Alzheimer's.[110] You have to learn to speak what is necessary, one concept at a time and to repeat as needed. Ephesians 4:29 talks about what edifies and what imparts grace to those who hear it. This means a radical shift in how to talk with our loved ones. With communication one needs to:

1. **Listen.** James 1:19 reminds us to *be swift to hear, slow to speak, slow to wrath*. This is especially true in dealing with our loved ones who often are not slow to wrath because they are losing some of their neurons in the hippocampus. They deserve our attention even when we may be stressed over the situation. It is our conscious choice to listen well.

2. **Learn to say one concept at a time in the right place and time.** Ken Sande writes:

   Timing is an essential ingredient of effective confrontation [communication]. If possible, do not discuss sensitive matters with someone who is tired, worried about other things, or in a bad mood. Nor should you confront someone about an important concern unless you will have enough time to discuss the matter thoroughly.

   Likewise, give careful thought to where you will talk. Unless it is necessary, do not confront someone in front of others. Try to find a place that is free of such distractions as television, other people, and loud noises. If the person you need to

---

[110] Coste, Joanne Koenig, *Learning to Speak Alzheimer's: A Groundbreaking Approach for Everyone Dealing with the Disease* (Boston: Houghton Mifflin Company) used by permission.

talk with is likely to be nervous or suspicious [as often with dementia patients], it may be wise to select a place where he or she will feel relatively secure, perhaps at home. On the other hand, if the person is known to have a temper, you may want to have your conversation in a restaurant, where there may be less inclination to make a scene.[111]

Speak the truth without deceit[112]. At times caregivers are called to offer "benevolent lies" to their loved ones. Rather than call it this term, the biblical term is "edification": *all things are lawful for me, but not all things edify. Let no one seek his own, but each one the other's well-being.*[113]

3. **Always emphasize that you have their best interest in mind.** Proverbs 31:12 says about the godly wife that *she does him good and not evil all the days of her life.* Romans 13:10 emphasizes that love does no harm and is the fulfillment of the law. Ephesians 4:29 says to let everything you say be good and helpful.

4. **Caregivers need to handle not only the anger of their loved one, but also their own anger.** Ephesians 4:29 says *Let no corrupt word proceed out of your mouth, but what is good for necessary edification, that it may impart grace to the hearers.* Ephesians 4:26, 31 and 32 encourages the caregiver to constructively meet problems: *Be angry, and do not sin. Let all bitterness, wrath, anger, clamor, and evil speaking be put away from you, with all malice. And be kind to one another, tenderhearted, forgiving one another, even as God in Christ forgave you.* Apologize in the moment when you are angry and fortunately because of the care receiver's

---

[111] Sande, op. cit., pp. 156, 157.
[112] Ephesians 4:14, 15 and 25
[113] I Corinthians 10:23, 24

short-term memory they will not hold a grudge. To edify you may need to get angry (or really assertive) at times for constructive directives to the loved one. At other times the caregiver needs to accept persecution from the loved one knowing that their reward is in heaven..[114] "Blessed those who persecute you", and "be at peace" we read in Romans 12:14, 18.

5. **Do not ask "Do you remember?"** Dr. Marie Marley, author of the book, *Come Back Early*, writes about Ed:

> A final example of what I realized was total thoughtfulness was that I frequently asked him if he remembered some event or person After months of trying to spark his memory of many events I realized that this was a stupid mistake. First, I believe it reminded him of his diminished capacity. Second, of course he wouldn't remember. If he would remember he wouldn't have been in an Alzheimer's facility.[115]

Master communication and you are on your way to adapting to the dementia of your loved one.

Routines and Activities

The heart of the prudent acquires knowledge,
And the ear of the wise seeks knowledge. Proverbs 18:15

It will take knowledge of your loved one. They have hobbies and pastimes. They are parents. They are consumers of movies and TV programs. It doesn't matter if they chose to vacuum the

---

[114] Matthew 5:11, 12
[115] Marie Marley, "Three Things I Regret—Are You Doing Them?", 1/31/18, https:// www.alzheimersreadingroom.com/2018/01/alzheimers-care-3-things-i-regret- are-you-doing-them.html, used by permission.

rug over and over again. John Zeisel writes: "I advocate treating people living with Alzheimer's as 'people' first and then as those with an illness."[116]

Routines are important early on and those routines will carry into later stages. Put things back where they belong according to the Alzheimer's loved one. 1 Corinthians 14:40 says *let all things be done decently and in order*. *Note also that the virtuous woman looks well after the ways of her household* in Proverbs 31:27. Be involved in the environment of the home and its safety.

Select wise nutrition from what they will eat as their taste buds keep changing. This is keeping their best interest in mind. For some reason many Alzheimer's loved ones enjoy ice cream and other sweets and often this can be used for behavior modification. Say, for example, "After we take our medicine, we get ice cream." My husband would eat his dessert first in a restaurant.

Socialization and activities keep the loved one active and engaged. Early on pay to have your loved one in a senior center they will get used to. When they miss you, have the staff call you and talk with your loved one. Tell the staff there to write them a note as to the exact time you will be back. At times photographs of recent activities and memories in the past help the loved one. They forget that they have socialized the day before, and you can let them know through pictures what has happened. Make weekly lesson plans almost as a teacher does for activities to keep them occupied and tell them each morning what they have to look forward to with a schedule before them. The Alzheimer's Association has a business card you can share with people in public (waiter in a restaurant, for example) to interpret that the loved one has memory issues.

The caregiver becomes the world to his or her loved one and it is essential to understand and accept that. Being angry at the situation will only make matters worse. When things take a turn for the worse, for example, the wise caregiver is prepared to take it in stride. Worries that caused consternation early on (such as

---

[116] Zeisel, John, *op. cit.*, p. 3.

not being able to drive) will resolve over time. Friends and family members need to come along side to understand and support the journey. "The" caregiver is the person whom the loved one relies on and that caregiver needs the mature Christian love to be there.

Just as dog owners are instructed how to communicate with their dogs through nonverbal means, over time those nonverbal communication strategies will pay off. The Alzheimer's Association offers bracelets and a booklet with these tips.[117]

- Approach from the front.
- Identify yourself and explain why you've approached the person.
- Maintain good eye contact.
- Speak slowly and calmly.
- Loudness can convey anger; do not assume the person is hearing-impaired.
- Use short, simple words.
- Ask "yes" and "no" questions.
- Ask one question at a time, allowing plenty of time for response.
- If necessary, repeat your question using the exact wording. People with dementia may only understand a part of the question at a time.
- Instead of speaking, try non-verbal communication. Prompting with action works well.
- Maintain a calm environment.
- Avoid confrontation.
- Avoid correcting of "reality checks."

Nonverbal cues mean that the caregiver needs to be trained. Teepa Snow teaches caregivers how to escort the patient. It is very helpful to view one of her videos.[118]

---

[117] MedicAlert + Safe Return Brochure, Alzheimer's Association, 1-800-272-3900
[118] Teepa Snow. See resources at the end.

Early in my journey as a caregiver, I was angry with the LORD because I had lost one husband to a heart attack and my second husband would die from Alzheimer's and there were so many unknowns as I faced this change. I withdrew myself from him emotionally.

One day early in the disease he said to me, *Carol, are you having an affair?*

I replied, No *I am not, Sweetheart. I am your devoted Christian wife and I am with you until death us do part.* I vowed from then on to not withdraw from Herb, but to be the same attentive wife as before this disease.

One day at church in our afternoon counseling course, Dr. Talbot went around the room and asked each husband what was his duty to his wife. I wrote down a couple of ideas to show him. He didn't need my input. He said when it was his turn,

The husband's duty is to be his wife's best friend.

And so he was and fortunately he did recognize me until the end and I worked gratefully at keeping my vows to him. Note that not all caregivers are recognized, but the unique mixed dementia that Herb had meant that he did recognize me until the end.

Special Caregiver Love

We are called to love like Jesus. The musical group Casting Crowns has a moving song entitled "Love Them Like Jesus" that includes these lyrics:

> You're holding her hand, you're straining for words
> You trying to make - sense of it all
> She's desperate for hope, darkness clouding her view
> She's looking to you

Chapter 6

Biblical counselor Paul Tautges in his blog Counseling One Another lists thirty-seven ways the Bible says to love one another.[119] Six are included with my caregiving notes in italics:

- Give preference to one another (Rom. 12:10). *Becoming the caregiver means that other relationships may take a back seat.*
- Accept one another by withholding judgment (Rom. 14:1). *Your loved one cannot help his/her disease and yet you can divert attention from the poor speech or behavior.*
- Forgive one another (Col. 3:13). *Someone with dementia will not remember what he or she may have done that was offensive, but you just need to be tolerant and forgive.*
- Comfort one another with the hope of Christ's return (1 Thess. 4:18). *Remind them of their faith in Jesus Christ and that when they die they will be with Him.*
- Seek good for one another (1 Thess. 5:15). *Keep them away from danger. They will not be driving and should not have access to weapons. They need safeguards so they do not wander in the neighborhood or drive off in a car.*
- Refuse to become resentful toward one another (1 John 3:11- 12). *This is the path that the LORD has chosen for you as a family member or as a church family member.*

As Tautges points out at the end of this blog post, you are showing you are Christ's disciple by your love for another (John 13:35). It matters we are there for them. Our presence is love.

---

[119] Paul Tautges, "Flashback Friday—37 Ways to Love One Another," 8/26/16 http://counselingoneanother.com/?s=37+ways+to+love+one+another, used by permission.

CHAPTER 7
WHAT OTHERS CAN DO

"What can I do for you?" others often say. Neighbors, friends, the local church have to be ready to help. Caregivers have to be ready to give an answer to that question. My friend Paula wrote on Facebook that she could no longer go to worship service. I devised a plan. She didn't think of it, but as a former caregiver I was creative. I called her and offered to "dad-sit" for her Sunday nights so she could get to a small group at my church Sunday nights even though she missed Sunday morning worship services. All the help I had been given for my late husband I could repay with caring for others.

Ministry to Caregivers

We are called to bear one another's burdens according to Galatians and Romans.[120] The 1993 the book, *Aging in Rural America* by C. Neil Bull, *recognized* the need for the church to help.

It is possible, or course, that there are a number of compensatory processes taking place, which buffer residents of smaller towns and communities from psychological consequences of rural change. These could involve psychological processes of

---

[120] Gal. 6:2 reads *Bear one another's burdens, and so fulfill the law of Christ*, and Romans 15:1 reads *We then who are strong ought to bear the scruples of the weak, and not to please ourselves.*

dissonance reduction or fatalism or they could involve social processes, such as increased reliance on the church. The elderly with Alzheimer's disease and their aging caregiving kin will become more recognized as "high risk" clients who are set adrift among the medical, psychiatric, and public social service agencies.[121]

Mr. Bull did not specify what the church can do. Larger communities have social services, but most all communities have churches that are called to care for their members. In whatever size church or community, the Christian needs to minister to the least of these, which include the homeless, prisoners, disabled and dementia care receivers. [122]

Pastors might assume that the caregiver is doing well, when in fact the need for support is just as great with any grief situation and widows are to be taken care of according to Scripture. If there is family to take care of the widows, however, the church should take care of the "real widows" without family.[123] Furthermore, there is a sense that the spouses of many care receivers are also widows and widowers in that they do not have the support of that spouse.

Thibault and Morgan are critical of how the church has handled ministry to persons with dementia and Alzheimer's. Dr. Morgan writes:

> I have found that the presence of clergy in long-term care facilities is rare. In my six years of volunteer work with people with Alzheimer's disease and other forms of dementia, I have seen the presence of only a few clergy, usually when death is imminent.[124]

---

[121] Bull, C. Neil, *Aging in Rural America* (Thousand Oaks, CA: Sage Publications, 1993), p. 114, 158.
[122] Matthew 25:40
[123] 1 Timothy 5:16
[124] Thibault, Jane Marie and Richard L. Morgan, op. cit., p. 144.

The authors reflect on the ageism in society and in the church.

> Both clergy and their congregations tend to reflect the prevalent ageism of our society. We have not moved far from the ageism of Shakespeare when he wrote, "Youth is hot and bold, Age is weak and cold; . . . Age, I do abhor thee; Youth, I do adore thee."[125]

Many seminaries do not train for this ministry, although some effort was started to advance gerontology courses in seminary by the National Interfaith Coalition on Aging in the 1970s that started GIST (Gerontology in Seminary Training). A 2007 study of this program found that fewer than 30% of seminaries are leading the way to equip ministers in older adult ministry.[126] Again, however, Thibault and Morgan have not specified what churches can do. Amos Yong writes, in *The Bible, Disability and the Church*, "that the church should be at the vanguard of showing the world how to value all people, how to receive the full spectrum of gifts, and how to channel what each of us with our diverse abilities has to offer to others."[127]

For this book, I called a colloquium of professionals together to brainstorm from their experience what pastors, laypeople and biblical counselors can do to help dementia patients and their caregivers in the church. It became evident that each situation is different and not all parishioners affected by dementia caregiving are receptive to help. The disease in their family embarrasses some parishioners. Nonetheless, this colloquium did come up with the following suggestions:

---

[125] Ibid., p. 145.
[126] Ibid., p. 147.
[127] Amos Yong, *The Bible, Disability, and the Church: A new Vision of the People of God* (Grand Rapids, MI: William B. Eerdmans Publishing Company, 2011, p. 146, used by permission.

1. Identifying people who are vulnerable adults or who have nobody else within the senior population.

2. Pastoral care team can become educated in dementia and know how to talk with demented parishioners.

3. Investigate denominational resources.

4. Plan for an aging population with the church facilities and church staff.

5. Use Stephen's Ministry for the care receiver and caregiver.

6. Cautiously leaders can make an assessment, asking questions of the caregiver such as: *What are your days like? How much extra do you have to do these days? How can the church help? Can we provide a meal or help around the house? Can we stay with your loved one while you do errands or get respite? Are there financial needs? What are your worries for the future? How can we pray for you? How can the church be a family to you now?*

7. Find out about community resources such as the Alzheimer's Association support group. Go to that group with the parishioner for their first time and provide an activity for their loved one while they go.

The issue is complex and the next chapter has some suggestions for meaningful activities that the church can use with seniors.

At times the pastor might be invited to bring family members together for discussion, prayer and support. Family, as well as others, do not walk in the caregiver's shoes and need to be forgiven as Christ has forgiven us when we misspeak or do not understand. Again, caution needs to be exercised with moving into the family dynamics and the Friedman triangle can help as mentioned in chapter two. Amos Yong points out in his book, *The Bible, Disability and the Church,*

> To be sure, in many cases accommodations will need to be provided, but the point is that the Spirit empowers willing vessels, not only those who fit some kind of conventional norm about what it means to be a minister of the gospel. Hence, the church should be at the vanguard of showing the world how to value all people, how to receive the full spectrum of gifts, and how to channel what each of us with our diverse abilities has to offer to others.[128]

Does someone sit with a spouse who has dementia, for example, while their partner is in the choir? It is important that care receivers feel accepted in the church family. They need to know people who may at times provide respite for the caregiver.

One unique example of what a local church can do is Trinity Place in Huntsville, Alabama. For more than twenty-five years it has been hosting day care for senior adults with dementia. More on some of their activities and other activities in the next chapter.

Challenge to the Church

Wear Comfortable Shoes by Peter W. Rosenberger is a popular caregiving book with this challenge:

> Church committees want to help hurting families, but shy away from "throwing money" at the problem. By serving as a safety net for caregivers who cannot afford medical visits, churches, for relatively small costs, can ensure the caregivers in their congregations receive preventative health care services. Churches may want to work with physicians

---

[128] Ibid, p. 146.

Chapter 7

and nurses in the congregation and even set up some type of semi-annual clinic for members (and even non-members) who are caregivers. That does not mean churches take over America's health care system, but it does mean that pastoral care can expand into this arena without causing a church budget to suffer. The financial component of the church underwriting a doctor visit is simply the last resort.

Why all this focus on the church? Because the church has a mandate for its head: Jesus. Societies, in general, recognize the need to care for the sick and vulnerable members of communities, but the church has a mandate to do so, and the head of the church is serious about that mandate.[129]

The author goes on to cite Matthew 25: 31-46 about the least of these and also James 1: 27 about vulnerable widows and orphans and we might add caregivers and their care receivers.

With my husband attending worship services regularly early in his disease and sitting under the preaching of the Word, I observed he was able to have that soul, that conscience, and maintain spiritual growth during his illness. One day at dinner, out of the blue, my husband said,

"God has a way of irritating you."

"How so?" I wanted to know.

It turns out that black edging was missing from the front yard. That edging had been taken up from a flower bed and left by the road. However, the trash pickup did not haul it away. I

---

[129] Rosenberger, Peter W., *Wear Comfortable Shoes: Surviving and Thriving as a Caregiver* (Nashville, TN: GrayPark Press, 2012) p.92, used by permission.

asked my husband if it had been picked up. At first he said, "I don't know. I must have done something with it." Finally he admitted he had put black edging strips in the cow pasture over the fence. His conscience was bothering him. I let the owners of the cow pasture know why it was there.

As my husband's ability to walk went downhill, Christians helped. Kenny Sexton helped my husband shower and a local Baptist church came in and installed grab bars. Then I got one of those cries this morning from the bedroom:

"I've fallen and can't get up!"

It was 6:30 A M approximately and sure enough he was on his rear end. I put in a text to my back yard neighbor Kenny who came over. I got on the computer and canceled substituting for the day. Two hours later hubby was in a non-emergency ambulance on the way to Plant City Baptist Hospital ER for another time of checking out my husband's ability to walk.

I drove to ER and I went into ER Room 7 with my iPhone and charger and had church friends and others praying. I texted hubby's adult children. My husband had a head scan which is standard procedure for falls with seniors and he hadn't fallen because of a **stroke**. X-rays revealed that there were no broken bones. His urine was checked and it was not another Urinary Tract Infection, although I didn't think so because he wasn't acting like he had when he had a UTI. Near noon hubby was released to go home. A nurse helped get hubby into our gas-guzzler car--so high up. She went to get someone else to help.

Nurse: How will you get him in the house?
Me: That's why we came to the hospital.

At home hubby got out of the car and used the walker and painfully made it to a spot on the couch where I usually sit which has a pullout for elevating one's feet. In our sectional the spot at the end was my spot and his was next to me with an armrest

Chapter 7

that slid out turning into a drawer between us. Now he was very partial to his spot of the couch, where he felt at home, so typical of a dementia patient. It was not surprising then that later in the afternoon, hubby longed for his "Archie Bunker" spot[130]. He got stuck at the end of the pullout on the unfamiliar spot, which we couldn't get to retract. There was about an hour of debating how he would get up. Even though hubby could have been comfortable watching TV with his leg elevated in <u>my</u> spot on our large sectional sofa, it was not <u>his</u> spot opposite his special coffee table with all his DVDs. He felt he had to move.

Kenny was not home because he was volunteering elsewhere as an Alzheimer's caregiver, but another church friend, Kerry, had kept in touch with me by text and had her husband Dave come by after his work to help hubby get up and over to his spot. In addition to the walker Dave helped him use crutches, which I happened to have to move the few inches. Now teaching someone with Alzheimer's something new like the use of crutches is difficult, but Dave was patient. Both Dave and I were SO surprised that all my husband wanted to do was to move to 'his comfortable spot"—the whole point of the debate and so typical of a Alzheimer's patient who has to have his "home". Having a sense of humor helps when you are a caregiver. The moral of the story is to just accept their reality and chuckle to oneself.

A year after my husband died on June 23, 2014, I moved from Plant City, Florida, to Huntsville, Alabama where I have family. I looked for opportunities to "pay it forward". I sat by a lady with Alzheimer's so her husband could confidently sit and sing in the choir. One day she left during the service to go look for something; her husband watched from the choir while I accompanied her out of and back to the worship service. When Paula could no longer come Sunday morning because she needed to be with her father, I "dad-sat" for him so she could get to a

---

[130] My husband had a favorite spot across from the big TV like Archie Bunker had above in the 1970s sitcom. Archie's son-in-law Mike "Meathead" once broke it, or once sat in it, etc. This sitcom chair was legendary, and I believe is in the Smithsonian.

small group Sunday night. I continue to find opportunities to "pay it forward".

Jesus Christ paid for my sins and out of gratitude to Him, I find things I can do in this life. I do not work my way to heaven—Jesus is my way. However, out of gratitude I find ways to serve.

Ministry to Care Receivers

It wasn't until I had to go to a nursing home myself that I observed what it is like for dementia patients who do not seem to have family. They need to socialize and staff are often extremely gush providing their excellent care for the residents' needs. While I lived there, I began chatting with them and singing with them. Coincidentally the church I joined here in Huntsville, Alabama had a prayer meeting there because my prayer warrior friend Virginia lived here. She used to have the prayer meeting at her house and cook dinner for everyone. However, when she needed a wheel chair and could no longer see our church prayer meeting relocated to Huntsville Health and Rehab. And we bring the light supper.

Now how would our Lord get me to my church's prayer meeting and the opportunity to live among dementia patients? I broke my two feet walking my dog! I slipped at a drainage ditch, fell backward, and the metal of the drainage ditch crushed the ankle of my left foot, requiring a cast; my right foot was also broken and it required a boot. So I discovered where my church prayer meeting was held. I still kept attending there and also visited my friend Virginia there, often taking my dog, Ziggy, who is a delight to residents there.

The authors of *Regenerating Generations: An Adventure in Vital Living* deal with senior ministry in the church and also conduct workshops for inspiring a ministry for seniors. However, I did not find them proactively addressing the dementia challenges that many seniors face in their book, although they might be doing

Chapter 7

this in their workshops.[131] Granted that ministry to widows can be handed over to the family as in 1 Timothy 5:16, which reads: *If any believing man or woman has widows, let them relieve them, and do not let the church be burdened, that it may relieve those who are really widows.* However, note that the church needs to be there for widows and the assumption is also for widowers. *Honor widows who are really widows* we read earlier in verse 4. As an able widow it was my concern to be there for Huntsville Health and Rehab residents and to keep up with the needs of our extensive church prayer list.

---

[131] Johnson, Evelyn, and Alan Foresman, *Regenerating Generations: An Adventure in Vital Living*, (Waukesha, WI: Reji LaBerje Writing and Publishing), 2016.

CHAPTER 8

ACTIVITIES FOR CARE RECEIVERS

Our loved ones want to keep busy. My partially sighted, wheelchair-bound friend Virginia loves to pray and sing hymns with me. She went out of town to a concert and I told her about a baby shower I was invited to and she invited herself! She lives her life and I often say to her (and mean it): "I want to be just like you when I am your age!" She laughs with glee. Retired missionary Naomi, who also lives there, loves to sing hymns, not impaired by her early stage dementia. This chapter sketches out what activities might be like in the home or nursing facility and concludes with insight from the colloquium in the previous chapter for what churches can expect when parishioners with dementia are worshiping among them.

At Home

Many of the dementia patients do not realize the path they are on and struggle to maintain a normal life. High functioning patients can volunteer and need to feel useful. The fortunate church with a Stephens Ministry or parish nurses can make regular rounds to visit the members in the home or in a nursing facility; Jake's Stephen's minister used to help Jake take care of Sally and Jake's yard. Here are some other suggestions.

- Find activities that each dementia patient will enjoy and has ability to do while they are able. Does he/she garden, read, clip coupons, watch TV, play a board game, paint, cook?
- Schedule activities early in the day to avoid sundowner's syndrome.
- Encourage friendships. Plan dinner dates or movie dates.
- Take a walk or engage in other physical activities. Go to the gym if that will work.
- Keep safe with activities planned. If the activity is not in a usual setting, be sure that the patient doesn't wander off. Find a park that is not by a creek, for example. Eyesight changes and the person may fall into the creek. Play golf as long as possible.
- If cooking, have someone there so that a fire isn't started in the kitchen because of short-term memory. Perhaps rolling out cookie dough will work.
- Have a quiet environment. For example, a bowling alley might be too confusing.
- Make the activities part of the volunteering for others. Fold laundry if that will make the person feel useful. Help fold bulletins with the church secretary.
- Put in effort to recognize contributions that are made. Give a certificate for length of time a person has been in the congregation or organization and mention what contributions they have made.
- Play music. Sing. Dance.
- Go camping perhaps with supervision of course. When you take any trip, someone needs to be with the person, and trips to the bathroom may be a problem for the spouse of the loved one.
- Sort clothes, poker chips or toys.
- Plant seeds and weed in the garden.
- Cut pictures from magazines; cut out coupons.
- Toss a ball back and forth.
- Roll up yarn to make a ball.

- Go for a nature walk.
- Play a board game or puzzle.
- Paint.
- Make a family scrapbook or photo album and label names.
- Finish familiar Bible verses or hymns.
- Help with cooking.

Other Places

In her book about the late President Ronald Reagan, *The Long Goodbye*, his daughter Patti Davis writes:

> With Alzheimer's, patterns and structure are important. My father has been on a steady plateau for a while now and his days are predictably structured. He comes into the office for a few hours during which some visitors are allowed to spend a brief amount of time with him. They shake his hand, have pictures taken with him, and they leave. His lunch is brought to him and he eats by the windows that offer a sweeping view of the city. In the afternoon, he occasionally plays golf or goes for a walk, always accompanied by Secret Service agents who have had to learn the mysterious choreography of this disease. It's a challenge to fill the hours for him. Holidays and rainy days are particularly difficult.[132]

Not everyone has Secret Service agents, of course, but as long as possible a normal everyday life needs to be maintained. That life can consist of what the individual likes to do. It will be a long time before they are confined to bed and there are many hours that need to be filled. Friendships will change.

---

[132] Davis, Patti *The Long Goodbye* (New York: Penguin Group, 2004), p. 179.

Chapter 8

The Trinity Place, a church-run Alzheimer's and Dementia Daycare, had the following "Structured Daily Schedule."[133]

Morning Routine

7:00 am – 8:45 am	Welcome: Coffee, Tea, Juice, Socialization Discuss News (Orientation to time/day/weather)
8:50 am – 9:30 am	DEVOTION & SINGING
9:30 am – 10:00 am	Body Recall for Fitness (Balance Class M & F Mornings)
10:00 am – 11:00 am	ACTIVITY (Cognitive / Physical/Coordination)
11:00 am – 11:15 am	BATHROOM AND WASH HANDS
11:15 am – 12:00 pm	LUNCH SERVED

<u>Afternoon Routine</u>

	(TOILET AFTER LUNCH IF NECESSARY)
12:00 pm – 2: pm	Quiet Time & WATCH TELEVISION
2:00 pm – 3:00 pm	ACTIVITY (Physical/Mental Coordination)
3:00 pm – 3:30 pm	SNACK
3:30 pm – 4:30 pm	ACTIVITY (Cognitive/Physical) SIT OUTSIDE
4:15 pm – 4:30 pm	Toilet Everyone
4:30 pm – 5:30 pm	Socialize, Prepare To Go Home

Eventually just eating will be a problem and many will have to be in a nursing home where pain and nutrition struggles are the main pastime. Carrie Jackson writes about such encounters in a nursing home:

> I knock on Dad's door, and enter. It's 5:30 p. m., and he has been up from his afternoon nap for about an hour I check the diaper supply and stock the fridge with Ensure. Dad is leaning back in his wheelchair, eyes closed, mouth open. I hear a moan, and I walk over, sit on the bed and take

---

[133] Used by permission of Director Liz Crutcher, Trinity Place, 607 Airport Road, Huntsville, AL 35802. Because of the 2000 COVID-19 Pandemic, however, this place closed.

his hand it's dinnertime, and lately Dad has been taking his meals in his room. Jeff brings in some soup. Tomato barley. I stir it, taste it, and scald my tongue. After a few minutes it's ready and I ask Dad to open his mouth. He does, takes a bite of soup and makes a horrible face but it stays mostly in his mouth. He chews for almost a minute and I wonder how that's possible. I don't see him swallow, but the chewing stops.[134]

Between these two examples, are many years and episodes and wondering how the disease will play out. How can their time be occupied at home or in the nursing home? How can the family provide meaning for their loved one in these difficult days? How can they support the care needed. Not all families can afford nursing home care and having a caregiver at a nursing home as in the Chicken Soup for the Soul example of Jeff, hired by the family to be there.

At Church

The colloquium mentioned in the last chapter came up with some ideas of what the dementia parishioner can do at church.

- Have a night out for caregivers and care receivers. Have dinner and a movie. At first the caregivers might need to stay for the entire evening. Then they can take turns staying with their loved ones. Several churches can go in on this night out.

---

[134] Newmark, Amy and Angela Timashenka Geiger, *Chicken Soup for the Soul: Living with Alzheimer's & Other Dementias*, Cos Cob, CT: Chicken Soup for the Soul Publishing, 2014.

Chapter 8

- Volunteer to stay with the loved one Sunday a quarter so that the caregiver can get to church.[135]
- Have the leaders become knowledgeable about dementia. Perhaps share videos from the Alzheimer's Association or from Teepa Snow. See list of some of Teepa's videos at the end.
- Have deacons or parish nurses make calls on the caregivers and their loved ones even if they are in a nursing home.[136]

In interacting with these individuals, certain rules apply. Do not talk down to the care receiver, but always stand in front of them and get their attention. Show them when you can. Teepa Snow has a video where she shows how to walk a dementia patient to a new area by giving them cues. Do not argue with them. Let them tell the same story over and over again. Let them talk about the past even if you know that the story doesn't make sense.

One church has a choir that pairs choir members with disabled adults and the group just enjoys singing. I met Fran while walking my dog Ziggy here in Huntsville; coincidently not only had I rapped for her son when I was his substitute, but also her husband died from dementia and she let me know that her church, Twickenham Church of Christ in Huntsville, formed a ministry for seniors to prepare them for events like Alzheimer's.

Activities can generate themselves from the unique needs presented. Do not forget to check with Sunday School and Preschool teachers for ideas. Sunshine Care Homes who do memory care as an alternative to assisted living write:

> Every one of us needs stimulation in our lives, and older adults are no different, even if they have dementia. Human connection allows us to stay

---

[135] Carol Noren Johnson, "My Turn to Give Respite," http://plantcityladyandfriends.blogspot.com/2015/11/my-turn-to-give-respite.html,11/21/2015.

[136] Batzig, Nick, „The Blessing of Visiting the Sick," http://www.alliancenet.org/ christward/the-blessing-of-visiting-the-sick#.VqqpJb4PlI, 1/28/16.

engaged with life and to enjoy new experiences. Though your loved one may not be able to do everything he/she was once capable of, there are still many opportunities to grow, learn and connect. [137]

Plan for exercise, mental stimulation, human connection and worship.

Sally and I and our husbands with dementia, did many activities together. Sally drove their van and pulled their recreational vehicle. I drove our van and pulled a popup camper. Both husbands sat in the passenger seat. We lived life as normally as possible for as long as possible. After Herb died, Jake started calling others Herb!

A Canadian paper picked up my travel with my husband from my blog. Soon I realized I would need more help to travel and then Kenny went with us, to assist my husband with bathroom stops.

---

[137] Sunshine Care Homes, Dementia, Alzheimer's and Memory Care blog, http:// dementiaandalzheimerscare.com/2015/11/04/why-staying-active-is-so- important-after-a-dementia-or-alzheimers-diagnosis/, 11/4/2015.

CHAPTER 9
DYING REALITIES

If your loved one has dementia, they will die unless Christ comes first. This chapter talks about what death is like for the Christian believer and how he/she can get ready for the transition to the new Heavens and new Earth we read about at the end of Revelation.

Essentially when our loved ones pass away, they go to a temporary heaven where their soul is with Christ. Randy Alcorn explains:

> Death is an abnormal condition because it tears apart what God created and jointed together. God intended for our bodies to last as long as our souls. Those who believe in Platonism or in preexistent spirits see a disembodied soul as natural and even desirable. The Bible sees it as unnatural and undesirable. We are unified beings. That's why the bodily resurrection of the dead is so vital. And that's why Job rejoiced that *in his flesh he would see God* (Job 19:26). . . Any views of the afterlife that settle for less than a bodily resurrection—including Christoplatonism, reincarnation, and the transmigration of the soul—are explicitly unchristian. The early church waged major doctrinal wars against Gnosticism

and Manichaeism, dualistic worldviews that association God with the spiritual realm of light and Satan with the physical world of darkness. These heresies contradicted the biblical account that says God was pleased with the *entire* physical real, all of which he created and called "very good" (Genesis 1:31). The truth of Christ's resurrection repudiated the philosophies of Gnosticism and Manichaeism. Nevertheless, two thousand years later, these persistent heresies have managed to take hostage our modern theology of Heaven.[138]

We are living in this world with Heaven as a glorious benefit ahead to believers. We will not have dementia in any form in Heaven, and we will reap rewards for our faithfulness on this earth. Because of Christ's death for our sins and His bodily resurrection, we will join Him in Heaven. Revelation talks about the New Jerusalem coming down to this earth and our souls and bodies will be reunited in a glorious existence and so "we will forever be with the Lord."

Sickness is a result of the fall of man, but the heartbreak of Alzheimer's and other dementias will be no more. We will remember Him Who died for us. We will remember our loved ones. We will enjoy life as it was intended before the fall. Randy Alcorn writes *"As long as God keeps you here on Earth, it's exactly where he wants you. He's preparing you for another world."*[139]

---

[138] Randy Alcorn, *Heaven*, (Carol Stream, IL: Tyndale House Pub. 2004), p. 113, used by permission.

[139] Ibid., p. 468. Alcorn talks about the temporary Heaven in his book, with the permanent Heaven coming when Christ comes back to reunite our souls with our bodies. But the deathbed is no place for theology. Romans 8:11 assures us that *if the Spirit of Him who raised Jesus from the dead dwells in you, He who raised Christ from the dead will also give life to your mortal bodies through His Spirit who dwells in you.*

Chapter 9

My Message to Dementia Sufferers

> *Those who take care of you know that His grace is sufficient with all the stress of taking care of you. You will not be in pain, but loved and led safely into the arms of Jesus. We can sing hymns. Your loved ones do not have to be sad that you are going to be with Jesus. Yes, they can grieve, but a better day is coming for the whole Christian family. 2 Corinthians 5:8 says that to be absent from the body is to be present with the Lord. He has prepared that place for you. It is okay to go there and our hospice nurses will make it easy for you. I love you.*

How Not to Die

Medicine has provided means to keep people living until there is a cure. Christ has already provided the cure. There is no need to freeze bodies until a cure comes. There is no need to prolong suffering when there is no hope for recovery. However, medicine wants to try.

AND SUICIDE IS NOT THE ANSWER. One Hollywood celebrity, comedian Robin Williams, who had Lewy Body Dementia and maybe also Parkinson's, reportedly took his own life because of dementia.

Death does not need to showcase expensive medical treatment to keep someone alive. A Religion Online article begins by noting:

> The fear of enduring unceasing pain, of being trapped by medical machines, of losing bodily integrity and personal dignity and of being an emotional and financial drain on one's loved ones—such fear lends strength to the movement for euthanasia and for physician-assisted suicide (PAS). Support for euthanasia/PAS has been spurred on by The Hemlock Society, founded by

former journalist Derek Humphry and based in Eugene, Oregon.[140]

Euthanasia and PAS (physician assisted suicide) have not been the Christian way to die and violate the commandment *thou shalt not kill.*

How to Die Biblically

Do Not Resuscitate (DNR) can fall more in line with accepting the time the Christian will depart this life. This is another means that Christians have always used to get ready to die.

Death is a highlight of life, not a tragedy. It's okay to die without those machines when the body wants to shut down. It is time, a loved one can say, and realize that a better world is coming for their loved one and that the LORD says in Matthew 5 *blessed are those who mourn.* The proper theology of death is part of that comfort. Alley Verhey says it well:

> It is easy, when dying goes badly, to blame the doctors, but it is not their responsibility to teach people how to die well and faithfully. That challenge belongs to the communities of faith. They have the resources and the traditions to reform our vision of death, to teach people how to die well and faithfully and how to care well for the dying. It is time for churches to rise to that challenge, to begin again to apprentice people in the art of dying well and faithfully.[141]

---

[140] The New York State Task Force on Life and the Law, "When Death Is Sought: Assisted Suicide and Euthanasia in the Medical Context", n. d., https://www. chausa.org/docs/default-source/health-progress/book-review---when-death-is- sought-assisted-suicide-and-euthanasia-in-the-medical-context-pdf.pdf?sfvrsn=0

[141] Verhey, Allen *Christian Reflection: A series in Faith and Ethics.* Waco, TX: The Center for Christian Ethics, 2013, p. 262.

Chapter 9

Joseph H. Hellerman has written a book, *When the Church Was a Family: Recapturing Jesus' Vision for Authentic Christian Community* and in this book he challenges the church to be there in instances such as death.

> Our uniquely individualistic approach toward life and relationships, so characteristic of American society, subtly yet certainly sets us up for failure in our efforts to stay and grow in the context of the often difficult but redemptive relationships that God has provided for us. Radically individualism has affected our whole way of viewing the Christian faith, and it has profoundly compromised the solidarity of our relational commitments to one another.[142]

Hellerman goes on to suggest a church family model.

Time for Departing

It could be that at the end of history if we are alive when Christ returns, we will not see death. However, for *we who are alive and remain shall be caught up together with* [those who died in the Lord] *in the clouds to meet the Lord in the air. And thus we shall always be with the Lord. Therefore comfort one another with these words* (1 Thessalonians 4:17, 18). Scripture comforts us about our own death or about meeting our Lord at the end of history and so we can boldly face our own death. In fact we can have confidence of the promised reward (c.f. Hebrews 10:35, 36). The late evangelist Billy Graham is looking forward to this great hope in his book *Nearing Home* where he reflects and even writes about his wife's passing:

---

[142] Hellerman, Joseph H. *When the Church Was a Family: Recapturing Jesus' Vision for Authentic Christian Community*, (Nashville, TN: B & H Publishing Group, 2009), p. 6. Used by permission.

Life can be like traveling a treacherous road. There are potholes that jolt us, detours that get us off course, and signs warning us of danger ahead. The destination of the soul and spirit is of utmost importance to God, so He offers us daily guidance. Some pay close attention to God's directions; others ignore them and speed past the flashing lights. But everyone eventually arrives at the final destination: death's door As people grow older, the less surprised we are by their deaths, which often come only after an extended period of declining health. There even may be time for family members to gather and be with the dying person in the final hours. That is the way it was with Ruth. "Her body is beginning to shut down," her doctor told me frankly. "Her death may still be some days away, but the process has begun, and you need to be prepared." Two weeks later we gathered around her bedside as her breathing grew more shallow. I was seated by Ruth's bedside holding her hand, and our daughter Anne was standing beside me. Suddenly Anne said, "She is in Heaven." Her breathing had stopped, and her hand slipped from mine. Her years of suffering were over; Ruth had entered her final home. Memories of those final months will remain with me the rest of my life: her growing frailty, her suffering, her expressions of love, our times of prayer, her certainty— and even joy—that soon she would be in the presence of the Lord she had loved and served for so many years.[143]

When the time moves towards death, the concept of palliative medicine is useful. Euthanasia and PAS have not been the

---

[143] Graham, Billy, Nearing *Home: Life, Faith and Finishing Well*, Thomas Nelson, 2011, chapter 6 of e-book.

Christian way to die and violate the commandment *thou shalt not kill*. Do Not Resuscitate (DNR) can fall more in line with accepting the time the Christian will depart this life. Medicine can keep someone alive, but God may be calling His saint home.

Verhey writes:

> The success of palliative medicine has led to great advances in pain management and to the risk of reducing suffering to pain and reducing care for the dying to the management of their pain. Dying without pain is desirable, of course, and effective pain relief makes an important contribution to the possibilities of dying well, but dying well and faithfully cannot and should not be reduced to a death without pain.[144]

Only if we can compellingly witness to our religious convictions about life, suffering and death will we be able to shape public attitudes toward death.

Deborah Howard, hospice nurse and author of *Sunsets: Reflections for Life's Final Journey*, emphasizes that we are told to set our minds on the eternal, not the temporary. We prepare by holding people with an open hand and trusting God for the endings. She also writes:

> Sometimes it is only in the face of death that people can have a true perspective. That may be when they begin to really see and appreciate life. They can distinguish what is good and valuable and truly important in life from what is unimportant and meaningless. When death forces a person to take a good look at life, it can also force that person

---

[144] Alley Verhey, Christian Reflection: A series in Faith and Ethics. Waco, TX: The Center for Christian Ethics, 2013.

to see God more clearly. At the very least, it gives them the *opportunity* to ponder these things.[145]

Our death is an event to which we invite special people in our lives. We tell them we love them and talk about our faith. An Alzheimer's patient may not remember to tell people *I'm sorry, I forgive you*, but he can tell those around him he loves them as they say this to him. Emotions are one of the last memories to go.

Mourning With Hope

Eyrich and Dabler write that we need to *adapt to these painful situations as Job did* and "choose carefully, thoughtfully, and prayerfully what you spend your time doing, and savor each activity, recognizing that you are doing it for the Lord"[146]. How we bring glory to God and live each day will be a major part of our preparation for dying.

When the diagnosis of dementia is in the picture, the family and church begin the process of early mourning. The church needs to be there for the family and support the death process.

Hebrews 11:35 recounts saints who through faith *were tortured, not accepting deliverance, that they might obtain a better resurrection.* In the meanwhile we need to heed Hebrews 12. We need to *pursue peace with all people and holiness, without which no one will see the Lord* and keep away from the root of bitterness (Hebrews 12:14, 15). We need to ask ourselves if we are leaving any unfinished business when we come to Mount Zion should we not live to old age when we come to the Judge of all.

But you have come to Mount Zion and to the city of the living God, the heavenly Jerusalem, to an innumerable company of angels, to the general assembly and Church of the firstborn who are registered in heaven, to God the Judge of all, To the spirits of just men made perfect,

---

[145] Billy Graham, Nearing Home: Life, Faith and Finishing Well, (Thomas Nelson 2011), chapter 6 of e-book.
[146] Eyrich, Howard and Judy Dabler, *The Art of Aging: A Christian Handbook,* Bemidji, MN: Focus Publishing, 2006), p. 26-37. Used by permission.

to Jesus the Mediator of the new Covenant, and to the blood of sprinkling that speaks better things than that of Abel (Hebrews 12: 22-24).

As Rob Noll notes:

> Century after century Christians rehearsed and applied their beliefs about death; throughout their lives they envisioned dying so that at the moment of death they would be prepared. They sought to die reconciled to God and their human brothers and sisters. They gave evidence of their faith in the life to come, either by professing it or by describing their deathbed visions of the heavenly places, often both. They offered comfort to surviving loved ones who desired to hear the last words of the dying who were so close to the eternal enjoyment of life with God.[147]

The caregiver and church needs to be vigilant in ushering the care receivers into God's presence. Death is not the worst thing that can happen to the dementia believer, and they can witness to the world the calm of the death of a believer. Palliative care makes the dementia patient comfortable. Hospice is called into the home or the nursing home.

Attitude towards the Death of Others

Biblical counselor Eyrich states that the responsibility for counseling is a role for every Christian as he points to Romans 15:14 *(able also to admonish one another)*; Colossians 3:6 *(teaching and admonishing one another)*; and verses in Galatians 6 which call us not only to restore each other, but to bear burdens and do good to all—especially those of the household of faith.

---

[147] Noll, Rob, *The Art of Dying* (Downers Grove: IVP Books, 2010), 21, used by permission.

Rob Moll writes about the history of death in the church:

> For nineteen centuries Christians in different forms and different cultures understood that their attitude toward death should be infused with hope, for they worshiped a Lord who had defeated death. They died and cared for the dying differently than others in pre-Christian societies. Believers created the first hospitals and ended flippant attitudes toward the deaths of the unborn, newborn and elderly. They created organizations dedicated to caring for the dying poor and widows. The first Christians distinguished themselves in Roman society by remaining in the cities when epidemics struck, caring for the ill and burying the dead when the rest of society refused to touch anyone who was ill. Though we modern Christians have undone their work, our early brothers and sisters in Christ brought cemeteries from outside of towns and cities into their center, integrating the community of the dead with that of the living.[148]

As Christian caregivers, we take up the same ministry.

Deborah Howard says that when we "deny the reality of an illness, we focus on what is false, not what is true When we do that in the face of facts that say otherwise, we not only deny reality, but we reject God's providence our hope is not in a miracle, it is in the Lord, Who holds our future."[149] Rob Moll quotes hospice doctor Ira Byock on the importance of family relationships.

---

[148] Ibid, pl 40.
[149] Eyrich, Howard and Judy Dabler *Art of Aging: a Christian Handbook,*Bemidji,MN: Focus Publishing, 2006, pp. 26-37, used by permission.

Patients who died most peacefully and families who felt enriched by the passing of a loved one tended to be particularly active in terms of their relationships and discussions of personal and spiritual matters. These families in particular also seemed to be involved in the person's physical care. In the broadest sense, it was as if dying from a progressive illness had provided them with opportunities to resolve and complete their relationships and to get their affairs in order.[150]

They are at peace with God and others. Moll also says that persons who can accept their own death and limitations model the life of Christ as was found in earlier times when Christians also cared for the sick and dying.

Isaiah assures us about our Christian loved ones: *But those who die in the LORD will live; their bodies will rise again! Those who sleep in the earth will rise up and sing for joy! For your life-giving light will fall like dew on your people in the place of the dead!* (Isaiah 26:19 New Living Translation) This will continue to happen until the last enemy of God is destroyed—death (I Corinthians 15:26).

Is Death Final?

Mark Twain is quoted as saying "The only two certainties in life are death and taxes."

Isaiah told Hezekiah, *Set your house in order, for you shall die and not live* (Isaiah 38:1). Solomon penned that *no one has power in the day of death (Ecclesiastes 8:8).* Psalm 90:12 tells us to *number our days* [so] *we may gain a heart of wisdom.* Psalm 90:10 says we have seventy years, perhaps eighty. Yet in 2 Timothy 2:11 Paul assures us that *if we die with Him, we shall also live with Him.* Paul wrote to the young Timothy in 2 Timothy 1:10 that it is Christ who put an end to death. John Owen penned a book called <u>The Death of Death in the Death of Christ</u>. The Psalmist wrote: *But God will*

---

[150] Noll, Rob, *The Art of Dying. Op. cit.*, p. 105.

redeem my soul from the power of the grave, for He shall receive me (49:15). We don't know how God will be glorified in someone's illness; it can be the miracle of healing or the miracle of heaven.

Again, Death is not the worst that can happen to someone. Isaiah 57:1 reads *no one considers that the righteous is taken away from evil* [when he dies]. Joshua talked confidently with the leaders of Israel: *I am old, advanced in age. You have seen all that the LORD your God has done to all these nations because of you, for the LORD your God is He who has fought for you* (Joshua 23:2, 3).

It was with that same confidence that the late Dr. R. C. Sproul read from Philippians 1:19-26 at his daughter-in-law's memorial service. The Greek for "far better" is really "much more"—superlative, not grammatically correct in English as it is in Greek explained Sproul. He could say this death of Denise was "far better" than for her to continue living. We do not mourn as those without hope, for Matthew 5:4 reads *Blessed are those who mourn, for they shall be comforted.*

Safely Arriving At Home

"Come Thou Fount of Every Blessing" is a classic hymn that includes these lines:

> *Here I raise my Ebenezer*
> *Hither by thy help I'm come*
> *And I hope by thy good pleasure*
> *Safely to arrive at home.*

Pastor Stephen J. Cole in an Internet sermon[151] reports the attitudes of Calvin, Wesley and Spurgeon toward death. John Calvin's friend and successor, Theodore Beza, was with Calvin when he died. Beza wrote, "We can truly say that in this one man God has been pleased to demonstrate to us in our day the way to live well and to die well." Both John Wesley and Charles H. Spurgeon were reported to say that their parishioners died

---

[151] Cole, Stephen J., Radio Sermon/Podcast. n. d.

Chapter 9

well. Spurgeon reported being with a dying tradesman: "I had a heavenly time with him. I cannot use a lower word. He exhibited a holy mirth in the expectation of a speedy removal to the better world."

A case in point is how my husband Herb died. Hospice had been called in to assist his dying at home. Hospice nurse read to me from the booklet. She saw the signs that the end-of-life was approaching and of course the Hospice policy is to make death as comfortable and humane as possible. He was dying, so gaunt, but the morphine made it so he wasn't in pain. Please understand this. It was time for a relaxing medicine and for morphine--every four hours. My Christian friend and neighbor, Kenny, who had seen deaths in his extended family recently, helped, giving those first doses to my husband--even coming back every four hours through the night. Another hospice nurse came out and he gave me further instructions on the medicine such as how to fill the syringes. I practiced this. After that nurse gave me confidence to administer the meds, I did--a very, very hard task for me.

The Hospice Home Care Aide came as usual. She is very competent but I also helped her. It helped me cry. He was awake with the bed bath and changing of the sheets and so I told my husband I loved him, Jesus loves him and there is a place in heaven, a home that Jesus has prepared for him there. He mumbled/mouthed that me loved me. This made me cry again because I was happy he communicated. My husband has been made comfortable.

Sunday night as he went to sleep with the morphine, I remember saying to him:

"Sweetheart, I love you, the LORD loves you.
He has prepared a place for you and it is okay to go there.
I will be okay."

That next morning, the alarm on my iPhone went off at 5:30 am to give hubby his medicines. Only when I woke up there was no breath and no pulse. I gave the medicine anyway just in case. But again a warm body but no breath and no pulse. Then I called the Aqua Team of Hospice and within the hour a Hospice chaplain and a nurse came out to the house.

The nurse performed various tasks including calling the funeral director. The chaplain let me talk. He also read from John 14:1-6 where Jesus said we should not be troubled because he was preparing a home for us in heaven. Thomas questioned this, even as every loved one questions death of a spouse.

Thomas: How can we know the way?

I had buried one husband from a heart attack. How can I go through his pain of widowhood again? How can I too go to my Father in heaven?

Jesus: I am the way, and the truth, and the life;
no one comes to the Father, but by me.

This is the essential good news of the Gospel. I have always known that since a child who at seven years of age remembers asking Jesus to be my Savior—HE is my **way** to God. But it occurred to me that Jesus is the way to navigate the choppy waters of widowhood. His **truth** is in Scripture. There is **life** that will continue and one day I will be reunited with all my departed loved ones in heaven. Then out of the Companion to the Lutheran Book of Worship he read this prayer:

> *Into your hands, O merciful Savior, we comment your servant, [my husband's name]. Acknowledge, we humbly beseech you, a sheep of your own fold, a lamb of your own flock, a sinner of your own redeeming. Receive him into the arms of your mercy, into the blessed rest of everlasting peace, and into the glorious company of the saints in light. Amen.*

After some time the black-suited funeral directors pulled up and put my husband on a gurney and brought him out of the bedroom. I had been carrying our dog Ziggy, and the men stopped by Ziggy and myself. Ziggy licked my husband's face and I kissed his cold face. Then before us they covered his head with the rest of the red cloth and brought him outside to a black van while I sobbed healing sobs. At midday the regular Hospice nurse came; she hadn't heard the news and we hugged and grieved together. The aide who had come most morning heard the news and she came also later in the day to be with me and we grieved together. Such a wonderful team! They let my husband slip gently into the arms of Jesus. He was ready.

> *You saw me before I was born. Every day of my life was recorded in your book. Every moment was laid out before a single day had passed.* Psalm 139:16 NLT

As a Christian I have that assurance also according to 2 Corinthians 5:8 that to be absent from the body is to be present with the LORD.

For Christians there is not such a thing as an untimely death, because our times are in the Lord's hands. Living as if this is our last day is perhaps the best preparation.

May we die well with time for spiritual preparation, repentance, last words to our family and friends, and reconciliation with God and others. May God grant us the ability to counsel our loved ones and church family on how to die well. Our journey to sanctification will be complete when we are with Jesus—glorious hope. Yes, it will be joy to rejoice and be with Jesus forever, to come home. We will need to communicate this to the dementia sufferer.

Charles Spurgeon said, "To come to Thee is to come home from exile, to come to land out of the raging storm, to come to rest after long labor, to come to the goal of my desires and the summit of my wishes."[152] We do not need to fear death.

---

[152] Charles H. Sturgeon, *Morning and Evening,* morning reading for April 25, used by permission.

Then I heard a voice from heaven saying to me, "Write: 'Blessed are the dead who die in the Lord from now on.'" "Yes," says the Spirit, "that they may rest from their labors, and their works follow them." **Revelation 14:13**

CHAPTER 10
GRIEF

Although I did not first think to write about grief with this book, Dr. Kenneth Talbot and Rev. Carl Malm drew these comments out of me. Some of the reflections come from my blog, Plant City Lady and Friends.

Just as dementia is different for every care receiver, grief is different for every caregiver. This is the death that is expected and it has its unique characteristics. The family will react differently than if it were a sudden death, but also they may not be as prepared for the death as you might expect.

Gavanndra Hodge wrote about grief: *Grief is the natural response to the physical loss of someone we love. 'Pain is the agent of change, pain is what forces you to adjust to this new reality. And it is also through pain that you heal,' explains Julia Samuel MBE, a psychotherapist.*[153] Hodge went to an acupuncturist eventually who helped her cry, get unstuck, and finally be able to experience joy again. Whether the dementia patient has been a spouse, parent or friend, this is the reality that has been anticipated all along with the disease of dementia and its prevalent form of Alzheimer's. Finally with death comes the reality of that grief. As Howard Eyrich points out, grief doesn't have its stages as in the Kubler-Ross literature.[154] And the myths of grief may also

---

[153] Gavanna Hodge, "How to Grieve," April 26, 2016, https://www.tatler.com/article/how-to-grieve

[154] Eyrich, Howard. *Grief* (Phillipsburg, NJ: P&R Publishing, 2010), p. 28.

not apply as Shawn Doyle points out in his book *The Sun Still Rises*.[155] C. S. Lewis writes: "No one ever told me that grief felt so like fear. I am not afraid, but the sensation is like being afraid. The same fluttering in the stomach, the same restlessness, the yawning. I keep on swallowing."[156] A grief counselor, Dr. Calm Malm, reviewing this manuscript asked me how I am surviving the grief after two years since my late husband died of mixed dementia. The short answer I gave Rev. Carl Malm, M Div,[157] is that I meditated on Scripture day and night—literally. I typed up Scripture that was by my side and even when my husband was in the bed next to me, I could review Scripture.

> Blessed is the man
> Who walks not in the counsel of the ungodly,
> Nor stands in the path of sinners,
> Nor sits in the seat of the scornful;
> But his delight is in the law of the LORD,
> And in His law he meditates day and night.
> He shall be like a tree planted by the rivers of water,
> That brings forth its fruit in its season,
> Whose leaf also shall not wither;
> And whatever he does shall prosper.[158]

I had much support during my husband's illness and even after his death I attended two sessions of Grief Share, a grief recovery group that included videos cohosted by David and Nancy Guthrie followed by discussion.[159] We were prompted to share a lot of our stories. I had the opportunity to attend a Hospice recovery program, but chose to attend the Christian

---

[155] Doyle, Shawn. The Sun Still Rises: Surviving and Thriving After Grief and Loss. (Shippensburg, PA: Sound Wisdom, 2014), chapter two.
[156] Lewis, C. S. *A Grief Observed* (New York: Bantam Book, 1961), p. 1.
[157] Center for Loss, Grief and Change, An Inter-Faith Ministry of The Huntsville Association for Pastoral Care in Huntsville, Alabama.
[158] Psalm 1:1-3
[159] For more information contact www.griefshare.org at PO Box 1739 Wake Forest, NC 27588. 800-395-5755

Chapter 10

Grief Share that was available to me. I blogged about my grief as I had blogged about my late husband's illness. I had prayer partners. None of the process of grief was easy, but I know first hand one can get through the grief. Perhaps the process in Romans 12:12 was a strategy that I kept coming back to: hope, persevere and pray. Biblical thoughts and biblical actions were my way to process grief as Howard Eyrich suggested.[160]

I had been a widow previously when my first husband died suddenly of a heart attack and had made mistakes as a widow then that I reflected about this second time I became a widow. A California judge, the honorable Tim Fall, had me write about my second round of widowhood on a guest post on his blog and in part I wrote:

> People are gifts to us, not possessions, for however long they are in our lives. When people or things become our possession, we are closed off to the spiritual journey of life; we think life is all about us—our rights—and what is owed to us. I am coming to say, "Blessed be the name of the Lord," as Job did when he lost everything. Christ's beatitudes included my suffering as a widow: "Blessed are those who mourn, for they shall be comforted."[161]

In this second round of widowhood I knew I had to quickly get rid of my late husband's clothes while I had help. My brother helped pack them up to donate. The king-sized bed we had shared was gone and Hospice had moved in a hospital bed. I had placed a single bed by that hospital bed so I could sleep by him the last few months. When he died, Hospice came to take out the hospital bed and I put a single bed in the middle of the master bedroom. It seemed bare and so I put other furniture in there

---

[160] Eyrich, Howard, *op. cit.*, pp. 36-38.
[161] Carol Noren Johnson as a guest blogger, http://timfall.wordpress.com/2014/08/19/ a-second-dose-of-widowhood/taken of f Internet now.

right away—made myself a sewing center. I was persevering and accepting my new situation as best as I could. Soon I had a sewing project that I would see when I went to bed or woke up. I made a quilt for the remaining grandchild of my husband; she had not received one as her cousins had. I sewed one of my husband's shirt pockets in the quilt. I made her a memory booklet.

My late husband had experienced <u>progressive grief</u> because he had to stop working, driving, collecting guns, and eventually did not use his cell phone or know how to use the TV. I silently grieved with him as I lost my husband's driving us around and other pastimes of marriage. He had some knowledge early on that he had this disease and would often enjoy his life but refer to me for the details of remembering. Even though I didn't want the day of my husband's death to come, I had been preparing for it. I had experienced <u>anticipatory grief</u>[162] and knew death was coming. I was ready for when my husband's spirit was with our LORD awaiting the resurrection of his body when Christ comes back to earth.

That day came. Christian author Randy Alcorn sent the booklets called "Heaven" taken from his book by that title that were distributed after the graveside service conducted by my pastor. It was summer and a family member of my husband objected to the graveside service in the Florida heat but my pastor backed that kind of service and officiated. This was the sensible way to proceed. (The funeral of my first husband had been very expensive for me and so I knew to keep this funeral simple.) My husband was laid to rest by his father—we owned the grave. Most who attended went back to our house for a luncheon and the eulogies and I had wonderful help preparing for that luncheon at the house—my family and my husband's sister. My eulogy was actually given in Toastmasters that next week.

---

[162] http://www.hospiceyukon.net/D_D_Anticipatory.html. This Hospice Yukon article gives helpful tips for family and friends expecting the loss of a loved one.

With his death I also lost his extended family because they except for a local daughter and her family, chose to say goodbye to me with his death. We had been married just over fourteen years, and with the exception of the grandchildren they had known him longer. His sister and family did chose to maintain ties and help with the lunch at the home.

Grief Is Not Easy

A little over a month after the funeral I wrote a quote from prolific author Anne Lamott where she muses about life, its meaning and the habit of people pleasing.

> "What if you wake up some day, and you're 65, or 75, and you never got your memoir or novel written; . . . or you were just so strung out on perfectionism and people-pleasing that you forgot to have a big juicy creative life. . . It's going to break your heart. Don't let it happen."

She gets it. She has forged a life as a writer. I am still trying to forge a life as a recent widow for the second time.

Here are my musings about my husband's death from mixed dementia that has jarred me into a new reality.

We feel entitled
It's all so simple
Uncomplicated
We spend to have
We collect people
To not feel lonely
We plan and expect
We think we have life all figured out.

Then life throws us a curve ball
Dementia strikes
Demands multiply

The loved one dies
But does not die alone
We are so glad to have
Those precious last moments,
They leave us with
That ever-present
Complicated grief.

It is we who are now alone
Our grief is complicated
No longer are we entitled
To our loved ones presence
To that special companionship
Things have little meaning
Grief is all the meaning.

But we are entitled
To forge a new life
Rearrange the furniture
Get out of the lonely house
To be with others
But it's not so simple
In time maybe
It won't be so complicated.[163]

My grief was raw. I felt it all over my body and all around me. A wonderful hymn by Brian Wren expresses raw grief:

When grief is raw and music goes unheard,
And thought is numb, we have no polished phrases to recite,
In Christ we come to hear the old familiar words:
"I am the resurrection. I am life."

---

[163] Carol Noren Johnson, July 29, 2014, "Grief Is Complicated," http://plantcityladyandfriends.blogspot.com/2014/07/grief-is-complicated.html

Chapter 10

> God, give us time for gratitude and tears,
> And make us free to grieve,
> Remember, honor, and delight.
> Let love be strong to bear regrets and banish fears:
> "I am the resurrection. I am life."
>
> The height and breadth of all that love prepares
> Soar out of time, beyond our speculation and our sight.
> The cross remains to ground the promise that it bears:
> "I am the resurrection. I am life."
>
> All shall be judged, the greatest and the least,
> And all beloved, till ev'ry hurt is healed, all wrong set right.
> In bread and wine we taste the great homecoming feast,
> And in the midst of death we are in life.[164]

I knew confidently that one day death would be no more. My husband and all my loved ones who looked to Christ would be cured; if you don't have that hope, you need to look into it and trust your loved one to the Lord. John Owens, author of the classic book on death, wrote:

> I discover the reader to peruse that one place, Rom. Viii. 32-34, and I make my doubt. But that he will not infect with the leaven of the error exposed, conclude with me, that if there be any comfort, any consolation, any assurance, any rest, any peace, any joy, and refreshment, any exultation of spirit, to be obtained here below, it is all to be had in the blood of Jesus long since shed, and his intercession still continued; both are united and appropriate to the elect of God, by the precious effects and fruits of them both drawn to believe any preserved in

---

[164] Wren, Brian, Hymn *When Grief Is Raw*, (Carol Stream, IL: Hope Publishing Company, © 1983), all rights reserved, used by permission.

believing to the obtaining of an immortal crown of glory, that shall not fade away.[165]

Such comforting words on the death of death!

But oh it hurt! Three months later I would write:

> Am I sad, depressed and grieving? Yes to all three at different times, *How are you?* People want to know. It's hard to know how to answer. My days of being depressed are less and less and I am weaning off of an anti-depressant (Paxil) now. I started taking it in May when my husband was going downhill. I take this pill every other day now instead of every day. In November I will take Paxil every third day.
>
> Having anxiety and depression is like being scared and tired at the same time. It's the fear of failure but no urge to be productive, and it's wanting friends while hating socializing. It's like running a marathon with the willpower of a corpse because you want to get to the end but you also want to sleep and evaporate into the soil and become compost for snails and flowers because then at least you're useful."
>
> No wonder I am not as productive as I usually have been. When I lose something or something needs fixing, it is A HUGE DEAL to me now.
>
> I am going to a Grief Share group at my friend's church. It is great to be there with others who have lost family members or friends. I can see those of

---

[165] Owen, John. *The Death of Death in the Death of Christ* (Carlisle, PA: The Banner of Truth Trust, 1967) p. 309.

Chapter 10

us who are sticking with this series are all getting better.

A discovery I made last week in Grief Share was that I am comfortable being a caregiver and have been reaching out to other caregivers now. However, being a widow is less comfortable. You have to eat out by yourself at times. You remember when you went places with your late husband. At home you remember his pastimes and think about how the home is different now, and what is comfortable as you forge a new life and changes you aren't ready for yet.

Tonight in Grief Share we dealt with what people say to us when we are grieving and how to forgive them with God's strength.

Grief is indeed complicated.[166]

Complicated Grief

When parents die from dementia, many new elements come into the grief process. What if it is hereditary? Did I, the adult child, do enough? Could my parent have had better care?

At times that grief can reflect shame and be turned by family members into accusations of the caregiver. Families get torn up over the process. Caregiving decisions and finances are questioned. When possible it is wise to get a third party involved to clarify; a mourning person is in no shape to be attacked by others.

I have had complicated grief when my mother died, but years later the hurt was healed as I wrote about it in my spiritual memoir, *Getting Off the Niceness Treadmill*. Not so with my late

---

[166] Carol Noren Johnson, October 7, 2014, "Grieving", http://plantcityladyandfriends.blogspot.com/2014/10/grieving.html

husband. Part of my processing grief from the illness and death of my late husband is the sadness that I am no longer part of his family reunions--by their choice, not mine. They didn't stay to hear my eulogy.[167] Having essentially processed this hurt, I chose early on to forgive. I now joyously enter into my family life in a new city with the family of my brother, his adult kids and their families. I have the privilege of many reunions without a long drive including birthdays and holidays and the joy of babysitting the next generation.

<u>Complicated bereavement</u> for a parent has been described by Barry Jacobs:

> This condition occurs when the normal grieving process of experiencing sadness and anger and then eventually recovering seems stuck. It's often associated with the development of major depression. That leads to the second question for her to consider: Have her many losses—including those of her mother, sense of universal justice, and grounding in faith—caused her to become depressed? If so, then it's possible her persistent anger at God is a manifestation of that depressed state. Counseling or antidepressant medication may decrease her depression and consequently lesson her anger at God. This may allow her once again to draw on her spirituality to find some semblance of peace about her mother's death.[168]

Certainly medication such as an anti-depressant can also help the spouse cope for a period of time, but the consideration

---

[167] Carol Noren Johnson, July 1, 2014, "Finally Giving the Eulogy for My Husband," 7/1/14, http://plantcityladyandfriends.blogspot.com/2014/07/finally-giving- eulogy-for-my-husband.html

[168] Jacobs, Barry J. *The Emotional Survival Guide for Caregivers: Looking After Yourself and Your Family While Helping an Aging Parent* (New York: The Guilford Press, 2006), p. 196.

should be made to also wean the grieving party away from the medicine. To stay on that medicine indefinitely means than one cannot process the grief and becomes stuck in grief.

Stuck in Grief

While you need to take time to grieve and that time varies, you also can get stuck in grief and not move on with life. With all the emotions connected with grief, the process of grieving may not be completed to restore equilibrium to the caregiver. He or she is used to caregiving, but not to a normal life. It may seem proper, even correct, to keep mourning the loss. The caregiver may have had that identity for as long as twenty years.

In *Normal and Pathological Responses to Bereavement* the contention is that "the smaller the amount of empathy the bereaved receives from those about him for coping with his grief the greater the possibility that he will become fixated in the mourning process."[169] In fact, counselor

N. Norman Wright suggests "If you're stuck in grief, find somebody to help bring you out of that. Sometimes we say, 'I can do it myself.' Well, at times the things we do by ourselves help us move deeper into the quicksand. So reach out and admit, 'I'm stuck. I need help.' Let the advice, wisdom, and encouragement of others bring you along."[170]

John Gray has another strategy for getting unstuck.

> People were stuck in so many ways simply because their past conditioning prevented them from recognizing and feeling one or two of the four healing emotions [anger, sadness, fear, sorrow]. I discovered that every negative state was the direct

---

[169] Ellard, John, Vamik Volkan, Norman L. Paul et al. *Normal & Pathological Responses to Bereavement* (New York: MSS Information Corporation, 1974), p. 45.
[170] http://reinventure.me/101-need-know-grieving/, podcast with H. Norman Wright, 2/4/16.

result of an imbalance of negative emotions. With the correct balance, a healing release automatically took place. Negative feelings were automatically replaced by positive feelings of relief, peace, love, understanding, forgiveness, and trust.[171]

Gray deals with the loss of a marriage through divorce as well as through death. He says that there are positive addictions that can help the sufferer get through the loss or to become unstuck.

> While it is healthy for men to focus on their work during a healing crisis, it is not so healthy for women. A woman has a tendency to avoid her own feelings by giving too much of herself. By focusing on her work or giving to others, a woman may become overly responsible for others and as a result repress her own feelings and needs. A woman should be careful that she doesn't lose herself in her work.
>
> Honest work helps a man heal his heart. As he succeeds in giving to others, the appreciation, acceptance, and trust that others give him actually gives him the strength and ability to look more deeply into his feelings and heal them.[172]

Care must be taken to accept and work through the grief. It is okay to get unstuck and to move on with one's life. It is okay for life to change—to not continue grieving.

Other grief happens before the actual death of the loved one by dementia. One is called <u>disenfranchised grief,</u> which is described by Doka as "grief that cannot be openly acknowledged,

---

[171] Gray, John, *Mars and Venus Starting Over* (New York: Harper Collins Publishers, 1998) pp. 41-42.
[172] Ibid., pp. 261-262.

Chapter 10

socially shared, or publicly supported".[173] Caregivers who see their family members and friends go downhill have begun to mourn silently. Soon perhaps their loved one will not recognize them. Doka continues "If feelings, thoughts, and words are left unspoken, caregivers may experience grief, remorse, and guilt when they suddenly realize it is too late to tell the AD victim all they wanted to say."[174]

People, meaning well, will say the wrong things to those grieving. *I know how you feel—my relative died.* They really do not know how we feel. *At least they're no longer in pain.* You are in pain. *Time heals all wounds.* It will take time, but that statement somehow seems cruel.

Moving On When It is Hard

A case in point. I had been down the road of widowhood before. I learned to let go early of items that would cause me trouble later— clothes and other effects. But now my dog Ziggy wanted to be by my side. He used to always be by my husband's side. Ziggy objected if I put curlers in my hair because he thinks this means I will be leaving the house. He has studied me and doesn't like those curlers. Ziggy sleeps with me and I realize he misses my husband also. He had traveled between my single bed and the hospital bed during the last months. Ziggy was there when the gurney came to take my husband's body, when I kissed his cold body and Ziggy licked his cold face. Ziggy knew. Now Ziggy needed a little variety in his doggy life, I thought. He had been outside in the fenced backyard for years while I took care of my husband but had scarcely been off of the property. He had yet to go on a walk with me. He didn't own a harness and a leash for a walk with me. (It seems to me that dogs walk their owners.) I also needed to get out of the house. It was summer when I didn't substitute teach. We went to Pet Smart and for the

---

[173] Doka, Kenneth J., ed. *Living With Grief When Illness is Prolonged* (Washington, D. C.: Hospice Foundation of America, 1997), p. 123.
[174] Ibid., p. 124.

first time Ziggy got to go in a store. He peed there by a shelf and I pointed this out to an employee. His vocabulary includes the C A T word and we went to look at the kitties and cats at Pet Smart. No match. As a matter of fact if you say "cat", Ziggy will want to go out to the backyard and chase that cat. From an excellent selection at Pet Smart, I bought us two items--the harness and the leash. Ziggy took very well to the harness and the leash and we first walked around a small retention pond on the concrete path. There was another dog there walking its owner and Ziggy realized this is just what happens. We passed some ducks and he left them alone. He trudged on until we found my car. Widows had to forge a new life also to deal with the reality of no longer being a couple. So glad I had Ziggy -- part of my therapy.

Within several weeks of my husband's death I did something strange that actually lifted my mood. I performed a rap in downtown Lakeland, Florida. It was impromptu. I wrote on my blog:

> Last Friday night, in downtown Lakeland, Florida, I volunteered to be at our Toastmasters booth, the first time I could do this. I talked with passersby's on the closed-off street about Toastmasters International and the local clubs. I told some that I have confidence to speak as a result of Toastmasters and, in fact, I even rap!

Across the way from us was a musical group, the **John Rhey Band.**

> I had the nerve to tell John Rhey himself that I am MC AC The Rap Lady on YouTube. *Could the band accompany me while I spit a rap,* I wanted to know. It happened. A crowd gathered and I just kept on rapping, not afraid.

Chapter 10

In the next twenty-four hours the word spread about this widow on a reprieve from her bereavement. Pictures went on Facebook and John Rhey and myself befriended each other on Facebook. I promised to pray for the band's career and his upcoming CD. He promised to pray for this crazy widow.[175]

It took almost a year for me to move to live by family in Huntsville, Alabama. I had help from family and friends. The downsizing and selling of my house was a challenge, but the move has been worth it. I now live by more family members and get in on their happenings and everyone's birthday parties. I babysit and drive family around in my SUV. All of these changes have helped me move beyond the grief. I have forged a new life, have new friends and don't have all the complications of the first time I was a widow.

What is recovery from grief? John James and Frank Cherry describe it thus:

> Recovery is feeling better. Recovery means claiming your circumstances instead of your circumstances claiming your happiness. Recovery is finding new meaning for living without the fear of future abandonment. Recovery is being able to enjoy fond memories without having them precipitate painful feelings of loss, guilt, regret, or remorse. Recovery is acknowledging that it is perfectly all right to feel bad from time to time and to talk about those feelings no matter how those around you react. Recovery is being able to forgive others when they say or do things that you know are based on their lack of knowledge about grief. Recovery is one day realizing that your ability to talk about the loss you've experienced is in fact

---

[175] Carol Noren Johnson, August 5, 2014, "Guess What Happened?!!!", http:// plantcityladyandfriends.blogspot.com/2014/08/guess-what-happened.html

helping another person get through his or her loss.[176]

Shawn Dole's book, *The Sun Still Rises: Surviving and Thriving After Grief and Loss*, covers the myths about bereavement that society puts on us and critiques those expectations. *What will people think? What is the time frame for grief?* He points out that the death after a sudden illness is not the same as a prolonged illness. One can get stuck not only in grief, but also in NOT forging a new life. "You will eventually be OK," writes Doyle assuredly[177]

Here are some gems from the book. Shawn advises to not have toxic people in your life.

- *I choose how I think and I choose my attitude.*[178]
- *Life is so short and precious that I'm not going to waste my life sitting around being miserable, mean, and sad. . . I choose to heal, honor the past, but embrace the present.*[179]
- Grief is not only emotionally draining, but also takes physical tolls on the body. We have to take care of ourselves.
- Get involved with others and give back to others.
- Decisions are more difficult when you are grieving. Listen to your heart, but also have advisers.
- The feelings of grief can include numbness, anger, distraction, nightmares, impulsiveness, special day blues, jealousy, lack of direction, lack of optimism, depression, and personality changes.

In chapter seven Doyle lists 12 rules of others and how to break those rules. He writes: "My advice to you on this rule is simply be yourself and don't worry about how you are supposed

---

[176] James, John W. and Frank Cherry. *The Grief Recovery Handbook* (New York: Harper & Row, Publishers, 1988) p. 7.
[177] Doyle, Shawn. *The Sun Still Rises: Surviving and Thriving After Grief and Loss*. (Shippensburg, PA: Sound Wisdom, 2014), p. 48.
[178] Ibid. p. 59.
[179] Ibid. pp. 60-61.

to or not supposed to act. If people want to misinterpret your actions as being inappropriate then that is their problem."[180] Doyle concludes: "Every day the sun still rises. You can either turn and face it, or hide in the dark. The sun is better for you, trust me."[181]

The SON rose from the dead so that I may have new life on this earth because I believe in Him and eternal life in Heaven. Christ said in the beatitudes *God blesses those who mourn, For they will be comforted.*[182] As the church has needed to be there for caregivers, the church needs to be there for widows.

> But he who looks into the perfect law of liberty and continues in it, and is not a forgetful hearer but a doer of the work, this one will be blessed in what he does. If anyone among you think he is religious, and does not bridle his tongue but deceives his own heart, this one's religion is useless. Pure and undefiled religion before God and the Father is this: to visit orphans and widows in their trouble, and to keep oneself unspotted from the world.[183]

If someone in the church has a widow (or by principle widower or other person in grief in the congregation), that family needs to minister so that the church can minister to those who really need help. "If any believing man or woman has widows, let them relieve them; and do not let the church be burdened, that it may relieve those who are real widows."[184] And God has promised to set the widow in families.

> Sing to God, sing praises to His name:
> Extol Him who rides on the clouds,

---

[180] Ibid., p. 118.
[181] Ibid. p. 170.
[182] Matthew 5:4
[183] James 1:25-27
[184] 1 Timothy 5:16

> By His name, YAH,
> And rejoice before Him.
> A father of the fatherless,
> a defender of widows,
> Is God in His holy habitation.
> God sets the solitary in families.[185]

We are told to *plead for the widow.*[186]

This World Is Not My Home

In 1816 Thomas Moore penned:

1. Come, ye disconsolate, where'er ye languish, Come to the mercy seat, fervently kneel./ Here bring your wounded hearts, here tell your anguish;/ Earth has no sorrow that heav'n cannot heal.

2. Joy of the desolate, light of the straying,/ Hope of the penitent, fadeless and pure!/ Here speaks the Comforter, tenderly saying,/ "Earth has no sorrow that heav'n cannot cure."

3. Here see the bread of life, see waters flowing/ Forth from the throne of God, pure from above./ Come to the feast of love; come, ever knowing/ Earth has no sorrow but heav'n can remove.[187]

Of course we need improved treatment and a cure for diseases such as dementia. But beyond that observation, is a greater hope. Heaven awaits the believer. The caregiver is a servant. Christ was a servant. Christ *for the joy set before Him endured the cross*. We are to count it all joy when we have various trials in caregiving.

---

[185] Psalm 68:4-6
[186] Isaiah 1:17
[187] http://library.timelesstruths.org/music/Come Ye Disconsolate/, public domain.

Chapter 10

The traveling man came home in the parable in Matthew 25 and received good reports from two of his three servants. He said to them:

> *Well done, good and faithful servants; You*
> *have been faithful over a few things*
> *. . . Enter into the joy of your Lord.*

Yes, you will grieve over the loss of your loved one. But you will have pleased your master. Romans 5 points out our *justification, peace, grace and* **Hope of the glory of God.**

The hope for the caregiver does not disappoint because God's love has been poured out. Because of His hope, the hope of heaven, we can be a caregiver and we can get through grief. I will see my loved one again. Maybe Sally and Jake, my sweetheart and I can take another camping trip together, enjoying heaven, along with others who have gone on before us! We will see our spouse again, but will not have an earthly marriage in Heaven (see Matthew 22:30). Instead, there is the MARRIAGE OF THE LAMB and all who know HIM are the bride of Christ (see Revelation 19).

EPILOGUE

After Herb Johnson died in 2014, I moved to Huntsville, Alabama where I have family. I did not expect to marry again, but an unexpected event happened that changed my last name to Patterson from Johnson (my last name in the first edition of this book).

My church prayer meeting was held in a nursing home by my Huntsville pastor, Dr. Randall Jenkins. Virginia, a member of my church lived there, and my dog Ziggy and I would visit Virginia often and even have lunch with her after church and the Woman's Bible Study when her driver took her out of the nursing home.

Why was the prayer meeting held there? Miss Virginia used to hold it at her house and cook dinner for everyone. When

Epilogue

she had to move to the nursing home, the whole church prayer meeting moved there Monday nights in a small room. Eventually residents from the nursing home came to that Praise and Prayer Meeting where we prayed for church requests and nursing home requests. We needed a bigger room and had to move to the dining hall after dinner. I would get there early and move the tables so we could sit around them. Then I would go to the rooms and nurses and I would wheel the prayer warriors to our meeting along with take them back to their rooms after the meeting. (See the end of chapter seven.)

This is where I met **Dr. Charles Carter Patterson**. I didn't have to wheel him back to his room like the other patients I helped. He had a **cane**. I thought we just had a professional relationship, this MD and I! After all I had written a book <u>Getting Through the Dark Days of</u> <u>Caregiving</u> and resident Carla Floyd had loaned him the rough draft.

Picture of First Edition

He started waiting for me to come back after everyone was in their rooms. He had buried his wife who lived in that nursing home—she had Mixed Dementia. My husband, Herb Johnson, had also passed away from Mixed Dementia. MD Dr. Patterson liked the manuscript. "Dr. Chuck", as I was introduced to him, had been a practicing family doctor, flight surgeon with the army, and in his spare time he played hymns by ear on the piano and painted--a distinguished Christian and renaissance man. He and his wife had even been to the mission field.

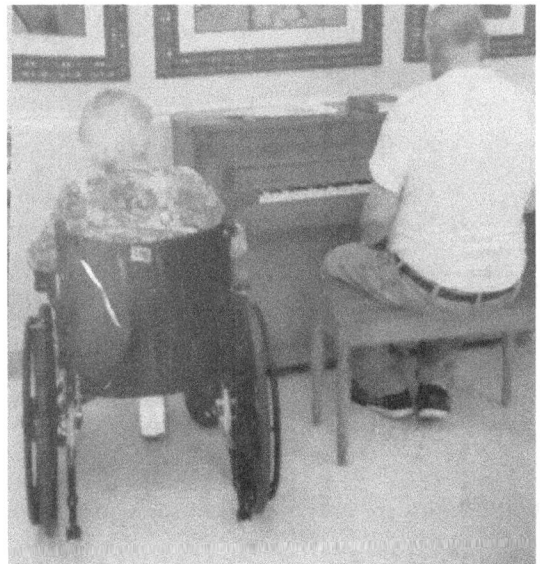

Dr. Chuck plays hymns for Virginia.

Dr. Chuck asked the nursing home to tune the piano and they did! Here is the story about how Dr. Chuck ended up in the nursing home. The Dr. called 911 when he diagnosed his own stroke (probably from the stress of taking care of his wife Jean). The ambulance took both Chuck and Jean to Huntsville Hospital. His adult children had both of them placed at Huntsville Health and Rehab, the only place that would take this couple at that time. Most of Jean and Chuck's Social Security then went to pay the nursing home bill and the rest of his property was distributed to his children; three adult children set aside assets for funerals

Epilogue

and other contingencies, expecting that both Chuck and his wife, their stepmother, would die at that place. Dr. Chuck's piano was given away and his car was given to a step-grandson. Fortunately, his local daughter Sue kept select furniture along with much of his paintings. Friends, Jerry and Lynn Kronk, adopted his dog Missie, and got other items. They gave back beautiful items to us, and faithfully visited us as Chuck's health went downhill.

Dr. Chuck and Jean were not allowed to share the same room. You will recall that I didn't put Herb in a nursing home as I wrote in this book; Chuck would note that when he read the rough draft of this book. At first Jean would live in another wing of the nursing home and she would yell "Chuck, Chuck!" Eventually the nursing home moved Jean and her roommate closer to Chuck and his roommate William. Soon Jean didn't know who her husband was.

Dr. Chuck experienced much anticipatory grief. When Jean passed away, my friend Paula and I went to the lovely funeral.

One day Dr. Patterson called his professional colleague (me, the author of this first edition) and asked me to take him to Bridge Street Mall. He wasn't driving anymore. I picked him up in front of the nursing home and asked him where he wanted to shop when we got to the mall.

"Kay Jewelers," he replied. In the store he sat down by the wedding and engagement rings.

"Oh no," I exclaimed! "I could use a pearl ring because I lost mine." It was my birthday and I thought that would be a fine gift, not knowing how limited his funds actually were.

"This is the right station," he said. It was a proposal! (Now I don't get many proposals! Had two husbands before and they both died.) We were the only customers there and the Kay Jewelers staff were fascinated with this romantic proposal from an older couple!

I thought *here was this fine man, MD, flight surgeon, painter and piano player-- a real renaissance man!* I saw his gifts of painting and loved his playing all the hymns that Virginia knew. So easy to fall in love!

We had one of his paintings framed.

I got up and kissed this gentleman and accepted the proposal! I called my Huntsville brother and sister-in-law and told them to meet at Metro Diner on Airport Road. My family were surprised and delighted with Dr. Patterson.

Pre-marital counseling was with Pastor Jenkins who knew us both from the prayer meeting. Dr. Patterson told him there were **ten** reasons why he wanted to marry me. We explained that we wanted a simple wedding at Central Presbyterian Church. No invitations—just Facebook notice and asking people in person to come to our 4 pm Sunday wedding if they wanted to. No gifts other than perhaps a donation to the Alzheimer's Association.

Finally, we started dating and planning our wedding. His daughter Sue started arranging a few pieces of furniture and his paintings to be delivered to my apartment. My brother Keith Noren would walk me down the aisle and for my third marriage his wife Ann Noren was my matron of honor. Two

Epilogue

family ministers were to read Scripture, two great-nephews to take pictures, and my friend Sandra Taylor to sing and Miss Eden to play her violin at the start. Ann and Paula worked on the flowers. Virginia and her driver had the guest book and cake and drinks were provided in the foyer. Denise, my Mary Kay representative, did my makeup and hair and we bought Chuck a suit (his clothes had been downsized when he moved to the nursing home). I would see to it that a fine gentleman moved out of this nursing home! All arranged!

Gary Rapp, Dr. Gordon Cash, Chuck, Carol, Keith, Ann and Paula Gattis

With Denise who did hair and makeup

Keep it simple but don't go to the Justice of the Peace to get married, we decided!

Epilogue

Nashville Boat Cruise

After the wedding and honeymoon in Nashville, Dr. Patterson moved into my spacious apartment. Dr. Chuck joined my church where I am told someone called us "The Golden Couple". We married for love and to fill the hurt in our lives having lost a spouse to dementia who didn't remember us at the end. We married "for better, for worse, in sickness and in health until death us do part."

I remember saying to this doctor, *neither one of us has dementia, neither one has heart trouble and neither one of us has cancer. We should be good for a while.* Neither of us drank or smoked. We wanted to make the best of quality time and eat the Mediterranean diet. He was my unofficial doctor. We got me new hearing aids. We got a handicapped parking permit so he wouldn't have to walk so far.

I continued substitute teaching some. Dr. Chuck had me get a tetanus shot when I bled from a metal door injury when a student burst through it. He had the lump in my breast from an old seat belt injury checked. When I was substitute teaching, I told Mary Peck, violinist and music educator at a school where I substitute, my new last name. It turns out she had been one of Dr. Chuck's patients. She said:

Dr. Charles Patterson was found by my father, who was going to him first. Once we knew the genetic lineage was important AND realized what a great doctor he was for our father, the rest of us siblings chose to come under his care. He made a huge difference in all our lives.

Mary was so impressed with him, and that I married him, and that I wanted to write about him in this Epilogue.

I had a chord organ that I donated when we bought a piano, a fine used upright Steinway with beautiful tone; he said *that's the one I want* when I played it from across the shop at A B Stephens Piano. We decorated the apartment with that piano, his paintings, his grandfather clock, and several other of his fine antiques. I painted dog Ziggy who met him during our engagement but died during it also.

Soon things started to go downhill. Did we need a nursing home or hospice? Two times he fell—once at the curb. The other time was in our main bathroom. I called 911 in the middle of the night to help him; I had been used to such happenings with Herb and I had even fallen myself and broken both ankles as I wrote

Epilogue

about earlier (what landed me in that nursing home for three weeks where I discovered my church Praise and Prayer Meeting).

Dr. Gordon Cash (best man at the wedding) came to our apartment to check on Dr. Chuck. Dr. Jeffrey Garber had been Dr. Chuck's doctor and vice versa. So, it came to be that Dr. Garber and I would exchange text messages about Dr. Chuck's health. Wisely Dr. Chuck wanted a DNR (do not resuscitate) and an attorney from my church, Bo Emerson, came to the hospital to arrange for this; I decided to trust the LORD and my husband about the DNR.

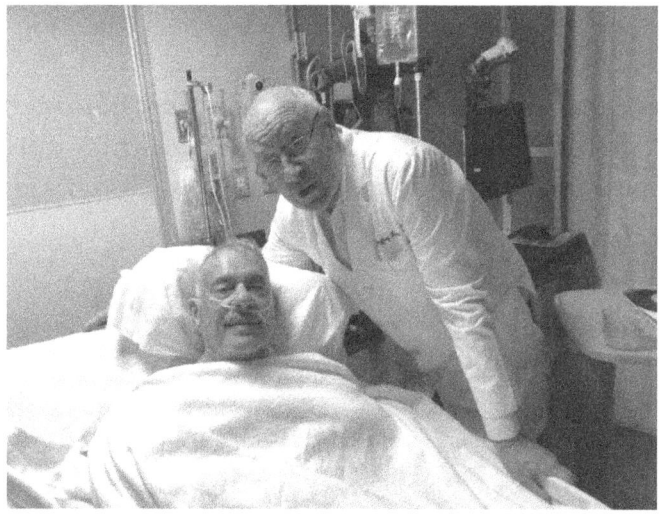

Dr. Garber with Chuck in bed

However, one night Dr. Patterson, who was now the love of my life, said to call 911. What started was a health and faith journey with Dr. Chuck. I stayed in Huntsville Hospital's Medical ICU or a regular room **even at night**. Dr. Garber came in his white jacket to check on him. Was it an aneurism? That could be cured in Birmingham. We called in the elders of the church to pray for him. Soon he was put in a regular room.

We talked about **palliative care** and his coming back to our apartment for therapy. Both of us saw nursing home problems. However, the hospital released him to return to Diversicare At

Big Springs Nursing Home and they had saved our room from when we stayed there before. They had physical therapy and we expected my husband would soon be walking again. Chuck asked me *Where do we go from here?*

"Sweetheart," I said, "we need to take one day at a time."

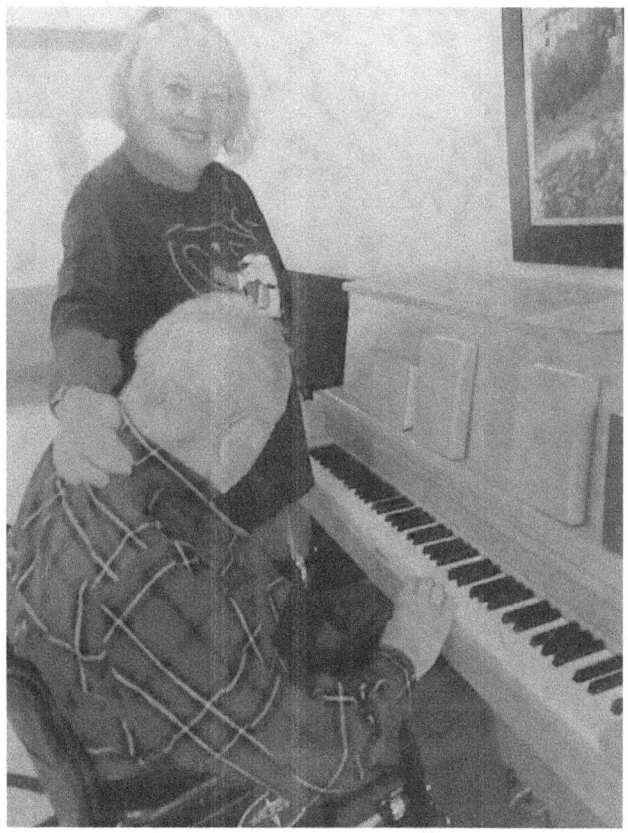

Diversicare piano where he was to play his last hymn "Turn Your Eyes Upon Jesus"

Epilogue

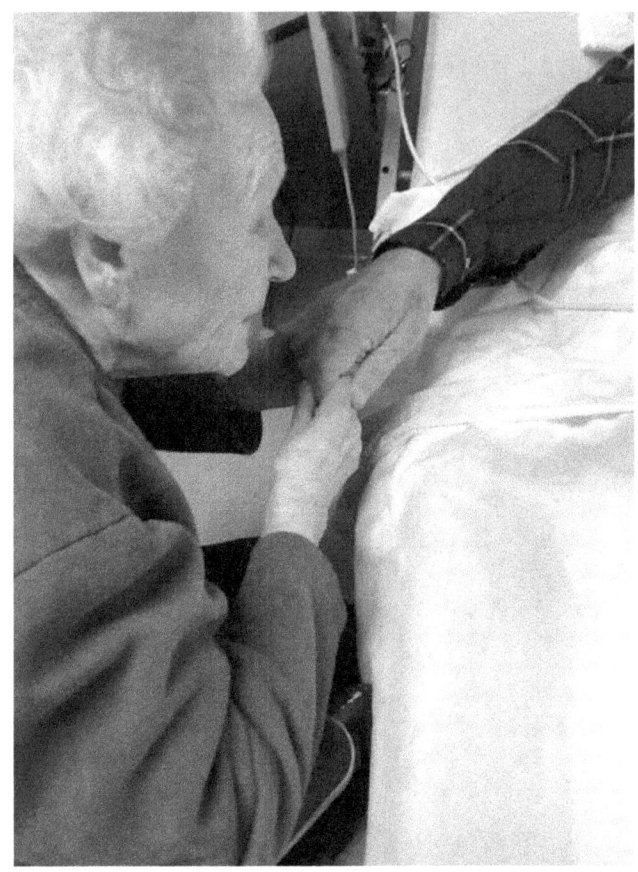

Virginia Uptain out of her nursing home pays a visit to Dr. Chuck in his nursing home where I am staying 24/7 with him.

It was 4 am in the middle of the night at that nursing home, our second stay there, November 28, 2019. "Sweetheart," I said, do you mind if I go to sleep in my recliner? I am SO tired!"

"Go ahead," he said.

Close to six am a nurse woke me up. ***Your husband is dying,*** she said.

"That can't be! He is getting out of here and we are getting him therapy at our apartment."

"Madam, no! He is dying!"

It was true and I watched him breathe his last breath at six a m. I ran through the halls crying and people had to calm me down so I wouldn't disturb the other patients.

Meanwhile our world has gone through the COVID-19 Pandemic. Had Dr. Charles Patterson not had a DNR he could have been spending this time on a ventilator in a hospital and I would not be able to be by his bedside.

Virginia was in that nursing home and I was not allowed to see her during the Pandemic in 2020. There was a drive-by event and I believed she recognized my voice (with her macular degeneration, however, she could not see me). What an amazing 101-year-old lady!

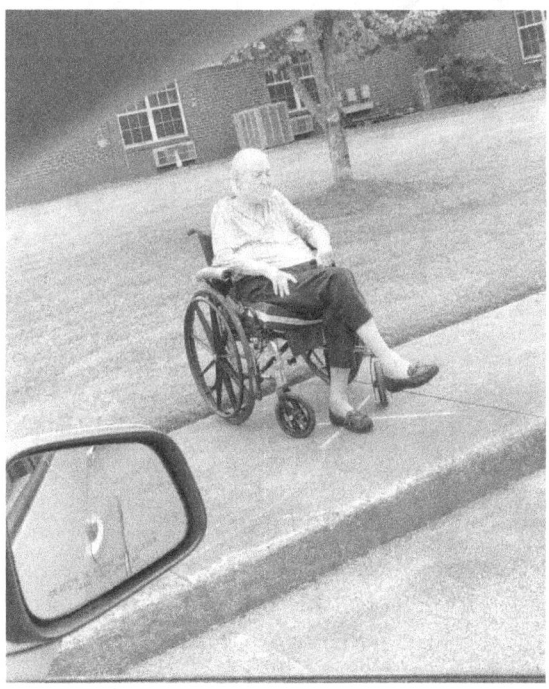

Last time I saw Virginia before she died.

Epilogue

Luminary

*Be kindly affectionate
to one another with
brotherly love,
in honor
giving preference
to one another.
Romans 12:10*

BOOKS CITED AND CONSULTED

Adams, Jay E, *Marriage, Divorce and Remarriage,* (Ann Arbor, MN: Cushing-Malloy, Inc., 1980).

Alcorn, Randy, *Heaven,* (Carol Stream, IL: Tyndale House Pub. 2004).

Brenner, Tom and Karen, *You Say Goodbye and We Say Hello: The Montessori Method for Positive Dementia Care,* (Chicago: Brennerpathways.org, 2012).

Bull, C. Neil, *Aging in Rural America* (Newbury Park, CA: Sage Publications, 1993).

Carter, Rosalynn, with Susan K. Golant, *Helping Someone With Mental Illness: A Compassionate Guide for Family, Friends, and Caregivers* (NY: Random House, 1998).

Coste, Joanne Koenig, Learning *to Speak Alzheimer's* (Houghton Mifflin Co, NY: 2003).

Cooley, Donald G., editor, *Family Medical Guide,* (NY: Better Homes and Gardens Books, 1973),

Davis, Patti *The Long Goodbye* (New York: Penguin Group, 2004).

Doyle, Shawn. The Sun Still Rises: Surviging and Thriving After Grief and Loss. (Shippensburg, PA: Sound Wisdom, 2014).

Ellard, John, Vamik Volkan, Norman L. Paul et al. *Normal & Pathological Responses to Bereavement* (New York: MSS Information Corporation, 1974).

Eyrich, Howard. *Grief* (Phillipsburg, NJ: P&R Publishing, 2010).

Eyrich, Howard and Judy Dabler, *The Art of Aging: A Christian Handbook, Bemidji, MN: Focus Publishing, 2006).

Friedman, Edwin H. *Generation to Generation: Family Process in Church and Synagogue,* (NY: The Guilford Press, 2011).

Genova, Lisa, *Still Alice* (Waterville, Maine: Wheeler Publishing, large print edition, 2009).

Graham, Billy, *Nearing Home: Life, Faith and Finishing Well* (Thomas Nelson, 2011).

Gray, John, *Mars and Venus Starting Over* (New York: Harper Collins Publishers, 1998).

Hellerman, Joseph H. *When the Church Was a Family: Recapturing Jesus' Vision for Authentic Christian Community,* (Nashville, TN: B & H Publishing Group, 2009).

Howard, Deborah, *Sunsets: Reflections for Life's Final Journey* (Wheaton, IL: Crossway Books, 2005).

Jacobs, Barry J. *The Emotional Survival Guide for Caregivers: Looking After Yourself and Your Family While Helping an Aging Parent* (New York: The Guilford Press, 2006).

James, John W. and Frank Cherry. *The Grief Recovery Handbook* (New York: Harper & Row, Publishers, 1988).

Johnson, Carol Noren. *Getting Off the Niceness Treadmill* (Lakeland, Florida: Genie Publishing, 2009).

Lewis, C. S. *A Grief Observed* (New York: Bantam Books, 1961).
Lloyd-Jones, D. Martyn *Spiritual Depression: Its Causes and Cure* (Grand Rapids, Michigan: Wm. B. Eerdmans Publishing Co., 1965).

Mace, Nancy and Peter Rabins, The *36-hour Day: A Family Guide to Caring for People with Alzheimer Disease, Other Dementias, and Memory Loss in Later Life,*, 4th Edition, (Baltimore, Maryland: The Johns Hopkins University Press, 2006).

McMillen, S. I. *None of These Diseases* (Westwood, NJ: Spire Books, 1968).

Newport, Mary T. *Alzheimer's Disease: What If There Was a Cure?* (Laguna Beach, CA: Basic Health Publications, 2011).

Newmark, Amy, and Angela Timashenka Geiger, *Chicken Soup for the Soul: Living with Alzheimer's & Other Dementias*, (Cos Cob, CT: Chicken Soup for the Soul Publishing, 2014.

Noll, Rob, *The Art of Dying* (Downers Grove: IVP Books, 2010).
Nudel, Adele Rice. *Starting Over: Help for Young Widows and Widowers* (New York: Dudd, Nead & Co, 1986).

Owen, John. *The Death of Death in the Death of Christ* (Carlisle, PA: The Banner of Truth Trust, 1967).

Petersen, Ronald, Medical Editor in Chief, (*Mayo Clinic Guide to Alzheimer's Disease* (Rochester, MN: Mayo Foundation for Medical Education and Research, 2006).

Piper, John, *When the Darkness Will Not Lift* (Wheaton, IL: Crossways Books, 2006).

Porter, Roy, *The Greatest Benefit to Mankind: A Medical History of Humanity* (NY: W. W. Norton & Co, 1997).

Rabins, Peter V., *The Johns Hopkins White Papers: Memory 2010* (Baltimore, MD, Johns Hopkins Medicine, 2010).

Rosenberger, Peter W., *Wear Comfortable Shoes: Surviving and Thriving as a Caregiver* (Nashville, TN: GrayPark Press, 2012).

Sande, Ken, *The Peacemaker; A Biblical Guide to Resolving Personal Conflict,* Second Edition (Grand Rapids: Baker Books, 1997).

Sheehy, Gail, *Passages in Caregiving: Turning Chaos into Confidence* (NY: HarperCollins Publishers, 2010).

Spurgeon, Charles H., revised and updated by Alistair Begg, *Morning and Evening,* (Wheaton, IL: Crossway Books, 2003).

Thibault, Jane Marie and Richard L. Morgan, *No Act of Love Is Ever Wasted: The Spirituality of Caring for Persons with Dementia* (Nashville, TN: Upper Room Books, 2009).

Verhey, Allen, *The Christian Art of Dying: Learning from Jesus* (Grand Rapids:Eerdmans, 2011).

Warner, Mark L *The Complete Guide to Alzheimer's Proofing Your Home* (West Lafayette, IN: Purdue University Press, 2000).

Westheimer, Dr. Ruth K. with Pierre A. Lehu, Dr. *Ruth's Guide for the Alzheimer's Caregiver: How to Care for Your Loved One without Getting Overwhelmed . . . and without Doing It All Yourself,* (Fresno, CA: Quill Driver Books, 2012).

Wright, H. Norman, *Reflections on Grief (*Eugene, Oregon: Harvest House Publishers, 2009.

Yong, Amos. *The Bible, Disability, and the Church: A new Vision of the People of God* (Grand Rapids, MI: William B. Eerdmans Publishing Company, 2011).

Zeisel, John, *I'm Still Here: A New Philosophy of Alzheimer's Care* (New York: Penguin Group, 2009).

FURTHER RESOURCES

Alzheimer's Association
(for general dementia information)
www.alz.org
800-272-3900
225 North Michigan Avenue
Chicago, IL 60601

SAY **NO** TO NURSING HOMES
Bottom Line Books
3 Landmark Square, Suite 201
Stanford, CT 06901

Grief & Share
(for grief ministry)
www.churchinitiative.org 800-395-5755
P. O. Box 1739
Wake Forest, NC 27588

Magazine
The Essential Guide to Caregiving
Centennial Media LLC
40 Worth St., 10th Floor
New York, NY 10013

Podcasts
Hope for the Caregiver
(American Family Radio)

Further Resources

Stephen's Ministries
(for training church helpers)
https://www.stephenministries.org/stephenministry/default.
cfm/917 314-428-2600 2014
Innerbelt Business Center Place St. Louis, MI 63114

Teepa Snow Videos
(for general demenia caregiver information)
https://www.youtube.com/user/teepasnow

YouTube raps by Carol
MC AC The Rap Lady

www.ingramcontent.com/pod-product-compliance
Lightning Source LLC
Chambersburg PA
CBHW071447070526
44578CB00001B/245